The God of My Parents

The Uncensored Account of My Journey to Find Identity

By Liz G. Flaherty

Copyright © 2015 by Elizabeth G Flaherty

www.lizgflaherty.com

All rights reserved.
This book is protected by U.S. copyright law. Copying, distributing, selling, or otherwise using any part of it without the express permission of the author is prohibited, with the exception of citing brief quotations for reviewing and group study purposes.

Scripture taken from the New King James Version® Bible. Copyright © 1982 by Thomas Nelson. Used by permission. All rights reserved. (NKJV)

Scripture taken from the New International Version® Bible. Copyright © 1973, 1978, 1984, 2011 by Biblica, Inc. Used by permission. All rights reserved worldwide. (NIV)

Scripture taken from the Amplified® Bible. Copyright © 1954, 1958, 1962, 1964, 1965, 1987 by The Lockman Foundation. Used by permission. All rights reserved. (AMP)

Scripture taken from The Message® Bible. Copyright © 1993, 1994, 1995, 1996, 2000, 2001, 2002 by NavPress Publishing Group. Used by permission. All rights reserved. (MSG)

First Edition

ISBN-10: 1512318981
ISBN-13: 978-1512318982

Formatting by Jack Thomas.

Cover design by Sasha Timen. (www.alookdesign.com)

Author bio photography by Johnna Lowery. Makeup by Olivia Lowery.

Dedicated to Jack and Ruth.

Table of Contents

Acknowledgments 1
Introduction 3
1. Beginnings 7
2. Elbows-Deep in the Country 13
3. Culture Shock 21
4. Giving 27
5. A Sandwich for Barney 35
6. My Date with Bigfoot 40
7. Mom's Book 44
8. Strawberry Milkshake 49
9. Crossroads 55
10. Peer Counseling 65
11. On My Own 75
12. Sinking Ship 80
13. One with Nature 90
14. Weed and God 99
15. The Narrow Path 107
16. Stretched to the Limit 120
17. Batteries in Africa 132

18. People in the Hallway 141
29. Out of the Limelight 152
20. One Lost Christian Walks into a Bar 159
    21. The Long Journey 167
    22. Dealing with Grief and Facing Pain 170
    23. Porn and Masturbation 179
    24. Same-Sex Attraction 187
    25. LGBT and the Church 193
    26. Unwavering Love 198
  Epilogue 201

Acknowledgments

First of all, an immense amount of gratitude goes to my husband, Andy. Thank you for believing in me, supporting me, and being patient with me every time I rolled out of bed to write something down in the middle of the night, or as I rabbit-trailed our everyday exchanges, often turning *what do you want for dinner* into a deep theological discussion. Thank you for being with me through all the struggling and the tears as I put my life to the page, and for encouraging me when I didn't think I could do it. I love you, and you're my champion.

Secondly, I want to thank my brother, Jack. Thank you for being not only my brilliant editor, but also my writing coach as I weighed everything out in this long process. I think we can agree that it was delightfully surprising how God brought this project together through us. It was a joy working with you and seeing your talents in a new way, and I can't thank you enough for pushing through with me even when the subject matter was difficult for both of us. Your humor and kindness brought me so much strength. I love you.

Thirdly, huge thanks to my friends who supported this project financially and those who reviewed the book before final publication. Without your investment of time and resources this wouldn't have come together, and I thank you from the bottom of my heart. Your prayers and support are invaluable.

Lastly, I want to acknowledge Lakeshore Christian Fellowship. Thank you for creating an atmosphere where people can thrive and experience the presence of God. You are abounding in hospitality and love. You are a treasure.

Introduction

I think most of us reach a point in our lives when we wish we could go back in time and talk to our younger selves. Sure, we would want to give them some lotto numbers—maybe the names of one or two companies to invest money in—but most of all we want to tell them everything we've learned over the years. We want to prevent all the blunders and hardship they're going to face. We want to give them the keys to a better life, which we had to earn through that same hardship. Sometimes it feels like just a few of the right words would have helped us so much. Well, unfortunately for us (and for our bank accounts) we can't go back in time. All we can do is take our experiences and keep moving forward. But even though we can't change our own pasts, we can affect other people's futures.

For a number of years now I've felt I wanted to write a book about my struggles and how I found my identity through Christ—precisely the book I would FedEx to my younger self if given the chance. I carry my testimony like a precious thing, and through it I'm able to minister to others. Committing my whole story to the page would allow it to reach people I may never meet.

Like many would-be authors I sat on the idea for a long time, telling myself that it would be nice to do *someday*, after I'd done all the other important things I was doing…like *not* writing the book. (This is one of an author's favorite activities.) My story and walk with God were conveyed to the women I ministered to, both individually and in small groups in my church, and for a time that was enough. Sometimes He likes to change gears when you least expect it, however, so one day while I was in the kitchen making soap for my body product business, I felt Him tell me that it was time to get started. I told Him I had a million other more immediate plans. He disagreed. So I set my heart to do what I felt led to do.

This book is the product of a lot of work, but it's also the product of a lot of living—loving, hurting, making mistakes, laughing, crying. It's the culmination of my experiences and the lessons I've learned in my journey through life. In the beginning I spent a lot of time praying about who my audience would be. I always knew that at the very least I was writing it to others who have struggled with the same issues I've faced, so that they could perhaps be inspired by how a loving God pursued me even when I wasn't pursuing Him. But beyond that, I was torn between writing to the Church and to those who don't share in the faith of the Christian gospel. Ultimately, I felt that in order to bring others into a life of God's love and Christian discipleship, you must have a people ready to embrace all others in whatever state they're in. My desire is to open up honest conversations and promote love and respect for all people. My primary aim is to un-vilify those who have been considered outcasts by the Church and to break the stigmas that I feel are keeping people away from Christ. This book is meant to inspire us as a Church to reach out to others with love and the good news of the gospel.

As flawed humans, we tend to create enemies and erect walls when others don't share our beliefs, and I want to show you how love and respect have built the foundation upon which my life rests—how that foundation is no longer based on fear. Regardless of who you are and where you're coming from, by reading this book I want you to go places you might not have been before, and meet people you might not normally associate with.

And you'll definitely meet some interesting characters in this book. Perhaps none are as interesting however as the little town I grew up in itself. I've changed its name and the names of most of the people and places, and I've made a few very minor detail changes purely for the sake of a concise story, but I can promise you that this is a completely open and honest account of my life. Full transparency is one thing that nobody *really* wants but everybody needs—a raw account of how God can move in our broken lives. Such transparency has been the key to addressing many of my most deeply-seated issues. Because of this, I've chosen not to hold back in an attempt to sterilize my journey. If you read something you don't agree with or even don't believe, I only ask that you finish reading the entire thing before dusting off the ol' pitchfork.

I understand that a non-Christian might pick up this book, and I actually think that's really great. Regardless of your beliefs, my hope is that it provides a perspective that surprises you. I'll do my best to define terminology normally associated with Christian culture.

With all that said, I hope you're impacted by my story. This, ladies and gentlemen, is me.

~ one ~

Beginnings

The gas truck pulled up to a weather-worn house on a quiet road in Morrilton, Arkansas. The truck parked on the street and a man stepped out. He walked up the short walkway and knocked on the door with a smile.

After a few moments, a gray-haired woman opened the door. The man was likely struck by the exhaustion on her face, and this impression she gave would only have been reinforced by the sound of playing children coming from within the house. (He wouldn't have known it, but ten of them had been birthed by this poor woman, and many had already grown and gone.)

"Hello, Mrs. Camp," he said, still smiling. "I'm here to fill up your gas tank."

The woman gave a weary smile and nodded. "Thank you," she said, and began to close the door.

The man gently placed a hand on the door and it stopped. "Actually I'm just going to need to make sure your connections are secure in your kitchen before filling the tank. It will just take a moment."

Mrs. Camp nodded and let him in. The man passed through the living room on his way to the kitchen, and by chance he happened to glance down at the floor. What he saw shocked him enough to make him stop. Lying on a blanket was a little girl, tiny and frail, so skinny that he likely wondered how she had survived up to this point. In fact, she only seemed to barely be alive at all; she hardly moved as she lay on her blanket. She looked old enough to walk and talk, but appeared to be incapable of doing either.

"How old is your daughter, ma'am?" the man asked. He attempted to keep his voice calm, but it was clear that his heart was sinking at the sight of this poor girl.

"She's two years old," Mrs. Camp said, and she sat on the floor next to her daughter with a smile. "Her name's Ruthie."

"She seems real small. Was she premature?" he asked, though he was already certain this must be the case.

"No sir. She came after nine months." Mrs. Camp looked lovingly down at Ruthie, who struggled to move. "She was two pounds born. We put her in a shoebox and put heated bricks beside it to keep her warm." The woman brushed some of Ruthie's fine hair out of her face and tucked it behind the girl's ear.

The man had seen enough. He serviced the tank, thanked Mrs. Camp, and quickly returned to the office. He immediately reported what he saw to his superior, and the two of them returned to the Camp residence shortly after. They pleaded with Mrs. Camp and her husband to take Ruthie to the hospital; otherwise, they would be forced to notify the police. The Camps did as they were asked.

Ruthie received the medical aid she needed, including several blood transfusions. After her hospital stay she began walking and talking. To this day I wonder if that man is perhaps still alive somewhere in Arkansas, possibly sitting in a rocking chair at this very moment. He would be very old by now, but it's possible. And if so, I wonder if he has any idea that there are people out there in the world—and in fact a whole legacy of people to come in time—who owe their lives to him.

The Camp family eventually left Arkansas for the farmlands of Fresno, California. Growing up the youngest of ten children, Ruth learned to be independent and self-reliant, even more so after the death of her mother when she was only ten. She was out of the house at every opportunity, and from a young age she loved being around people above all things. After graduating from high school she thrived as a waitress at Bob's Big Boy, and when she wasn't working she was zipping around California in her beat-up MG sports car, visiting friends.

Unfortunately, her medical problems would never be fully behind her. Throughout her childhood and into her twenties she would have fainting spells. On many occasions she would be sent home from school because of them, but the affliction went long-undiagnosed. Her father accused her of faking her issues and made no effort to help. It wasn't until her early twenties that one of her spells landed her in the hospital, and the doctors discovered that one of her kidneys had failed completely and was filled with toxins. Had it been left just a little longer to erupt, she would have died. Yet another close call that could have cut this story very short. God's hand was on my mother's life, and thus on my own as well, before I was even born.

After recovering, Ruth transferred to a Bob's Big Boy in Mountain View, then scored a position at Hewlett Packard—one that provided training and benefits. It was her first major job. (Ah, to live in the 70's...)

Jack was born into a family of fifth-generation Christians. Ministry ran in their blood; his mother would tell stories about how their forebears would travel through the coal mining mountains and fields of Virginia, teaching the gospel to anyone who would hear it. There was a long legacy of provision as well. Whole bags of groceries mysteriously showing up on the porch right when the food ran out in the middle of a long winter, with no tracks in the snow—that sort of thing.

Young Jack was perhaps the polar opposite of Ruth—quiet, reserved, somewhat shy, with a very subtle sense of humor. His father was in the Air Force, and as such the family moved often. Jack stayed at home into his twenties, and when they landed in Sacramento, California he moved into his first apartment.

One day at a church friend's house he met Ruth, who was visiting from Mountain View. They instantly hit it off and wrote letters to each other for several months. And a mere six months after moving out on his own, he married her, moved to Mountain View, and took a job at Hewlett Packard as well. Three years later, in the fall of 1978, a blonde-haired, blue-eyed, sassy-pants little girl came into the picture. And that's where my story begins.

The three of us lived in a little apartment with an avocado tree outside. I went to a private Christian school, and my parents made a lot of money at HP. Things were good, and I did enjoy being an only child, but I still prayed for a sibling every night before bed. It became as much a ritual as brushing my teeth or taking a bath. What I wasn't aware of however, was that my mother's health problems had followed her into parenthood; my birth was followed by three miscarriages, and the doctors told her that her body would simply be unable to produce a second child. But even had I known that, I wouldn't have stopped praying every single night.

I was seven years old in the summer of 1986 when my parents left their high-paying jobs in Silicon Valley to follow what my father referred to as "the call of God." Both of them felt called to pastor a small church in the sleepy mountains of Northern California. A four-hour drive up the highway took us away from our safe little Bay Area community and our secure incomes and into the redwoods. All at once we were in a place where religious and political views varied enormously from our own—where the very people who walked the streets were very different from us, where almost every aspect of life felt new and strange. Mountain View was by no means a sprawling metropolis, but comparatively, Wilsonville felt like a dollhouse. The bulk of the town lay along a stretch of highway hardly a mile long, if that, with most of the whopping twelve hundred residents nestled in the mountains and woods surrounding it.

Suffice it to say, Mom and Dad had brought me to a strange place.

The church matched the town perfectly—strikingly small, one legendary Easter fitting seventy people at its max, but over the years averaging thirty or fewer per week. At the outset there were five members on the books. Immediately across the street was Wilsonville's only public elementary school, which connected to the middle school, with the high school only a few blocks from there. A short concrete path led from the church to the modest two-bedroom parsonage next door. This was provided for us by the denominational headquarters, which managed the church. Unfortunately, in addition to being small, both the house and the church were on the verge of being condemned when we first arrived. Over several years, my grandparents drove from Oklahoma to spend summer months working on the two buildings in order to make them more livable. My grandfather recalled that one of the first issues to require a fix was big holes in the floor and walls where nests of hornets had made their homes; some previous tenant had most ingeniously hammered mason jar lids over some of the openings to try and stop them from crumbling further. The denominational headquarters would also offer time and effort to help fix the place up, and over the years the house would basically be rebuilt in its entirety.

Arriving in Wilsonville for the first time was a culture shock to say the least, and a lot for my seven-year-old mind to take; the idea of attending a new school was particularly terrifying. A low level of anxiety took root inside me, and for the first time in my short life the future was an uncertain mystery.

For a number of years those roots would only grow. It was the beginning of a long journey.

two

Elbows-Deep in the Country

My parents drove around town, taking in the sights, and I rode along in the back seat. We had just moved in and wanted to familiarize ourselves with the town's different businesses and landmarks. It was a short drive.

When we were done, Dad coasted past the elementary school before pulling into our driveway (which again, was *directly* across the street). I leaned forward in my seat and grabbed my mom's shoulder as we both watched the little school go by.

"I don't want to go there, Mom," I said.

She smiled back at me. "Well, we have a couple of months to look at other options." She and Dad exchanged a quick look. They both knew that in a town of twelve hundred people the options would be limited.

There were plenty of reasons to be afraid of the school, at least from our perspective. A lady in church had told my mom about the time that one of the teachers brought in a blood-filled placenta, donated after one of Wilsonville's residents had given a home birth. There were other reasons as well, but even if this had been the only one, it was more than enough.

"Yes, and the teacher put her hand down into it!" Mom had gagged on her coffee when she recounted the tale to me. I had run to my room. At the age of seven I didn't know what a placenta was, but I knew that anything filled with blood could only mean bad business.

After hearing such a tall tale I began to get my affairs in order and planned my move back to Mountain View. Back to my private Christian school, and the nice apartment. Back to our big church where I had lots of Christian friends. None of this placenta stuff. I mean, where the heck had we ended up? The moving itself had been bad enough, but now we were dealing with blood. Blood, and hands in blood. No deal. It's a silly story, but it marks a time when I began to develop a fear-based understanding of our new community. I jumped to conclusions instead of actually seeking out any real information.

Much to our unanimous relief we did manage to find a private Christian school that was starting up a few miles out of town. Being holy-rolling Pentecostals, we were a little concerned about the fact that it was…well, we'll just call it a "non-Pentecostal" school. A *very* non-Pentecostal school. But we were officially out of options, so I enrolled. We had to wear uniforms, because having a student body consisting of eight kids ranging from the ages of seven to sixteen tends to create too much tension, and the staff was rightfully afraid of gang violence…

Okay, I really couldn't tell you why we needed to wear uniforms. We lived out in the sticks, for Pete's sake.

On my first day, before sending me off to battle the Crips in my red vest and pigtails, my dad sat me down. "Now honey," he said, "we have different beliefs than the school does, but we're going to focus on what we have in common. So please don't bring up things like the gifts of the spirit and speaking in tongues and all that, okay? We want to be respectful." He tied my shoes and kissed me.

The school was a three-bedroom rental house that sat on an expanse of beautiful fields. Cattle and elk roamed freely in the pasture behind the school. Each student had his or her own cubicle to work in, and these lined the walls of the living room. In the middle of the room was a tall wooden desk that had been custom built for this odd little school. Within it were the answer keys for each chapter of our reading material.

We started that lovely first day with a list of hard instructions from the teacher, a thin, tall woman: "You are to do your work quietly, and you're not allowed to talk to each other." She held up three small flags in turn—the American flag, a Christian flag with a cross in the corner, and the bear-adorned flag of California. "These are to be used when you have a question, when you need to use the restroom, and when you wish to get up and check your work with an answer key." I looked up and saw the little flag holders on top of each cubicle. "Also," she continued, "we will be using the demerit method of discipline." At this she seemed to scan the room for the weakest among us. To me, the demerit method sounded very painful. Like little pitchforks that got thrown at your face when you told a lie or something.

"There will be a demerit given for leaving your cubicle without being dismissed, for talking to another classmate, for forgetting to take your flag down after your question is answered, for…"

At that point my mind went to a happy place. I needed some time before I could absorb any more of this. Fortunately after the rules were written onto a stone tablet with the blood of a lamb, we were allowed to mingle for a bit before being assigned to our cubicles. One of the kinder members of the staff walked up to me and led me to my seat.

"Now, I trust you won't sit here and daydream all day," he said with a small grin. I didn't know what he meant at first, but I was forced to hold back a grin of my own when I reached my cubicle. It was the only one built around a window, and it looked out over the gorgeous field. And it was in the corner, away from the other non-Pentecostals to boot! I instantly thought, *What a fabulous idea! I love to daydream!* I would spend a lot of time staring out that window. Heck, most of this book was written between bouts of staring out my office window.

Physical Education consisted of either playing in the back yard with whatever balls had been donated to the school or walking the perimeter of the property, which ran a couple of miles. Being on the chunky side I naturally avoided the walk for as long as I could, but eventually they ordered us to walk the entire circuit as a group. It was all I could do just to keep my chubby legs moving, and after a while I was pretty used to being about twenty feet behind the rest of the pack at all times. About halfway through our walk I saw that the kids up ahead were stopped at a section of fence. When I managed to catch up I saw that they were looking at what appeared to be a fawn lying in the open space under the fence. It looked like it might have been stuck, but we couldn't tell.

One of the girls pondered the sight, then pointed down at the little creature. "You know," she said, "that doesn't look like a deer's face. That looks like an elk's face."

Right at that moment one of the boys in the group pointed behind us and screamed, "ELK! ELK!" We all turned to find a large, fully-horned elk bull charging right at us! My heart stopped and a cloud of dust rose up around me as the others ran for their lives. I tried to run after them…but when the dust settled I was still in the same spot with my fists clenched and my eyes closed. Fortunately one of the older girls ran back and started shoving me from behind, like she was trying to tip a cow. Tears streaming down my face, still not wanting to look and see if the elk was advancing on us, I managed to get running—albeit in something like slow motion. My life flashed before my eyes as I trundled awkwardly down the path, red in the face, babbling incoherently. My parents, my friends, Jelly Bellies… All of it was going to be gone! *Don't die, Liz!* the little Liz inside of me screamed. *There's too much to live for!*

Finally we arrived back at the house. No one had been injured and the affair was over…but my fear of elk began on that day. My fear of elk, and my fear of running from them.

I spent many boring days in that little cubicle, staring shamelessly out over the field. But on one particular afternoon not even the thrill of watching grass grow could assuage my boredom. In that compulsive yet casual way in which the mind of a child will suddenly grab onto an idea regardless of how bad it is, I decided to shake things up a bit during one of our breaks.

We were chatting while the teacher was out of the room and I wasted no time in making my move. "So, um," I began in what I hoped was a casual manner, "you guys don't believe in the gifts of the spirit?" The moment the last word was out of my mouth I could tell by the looks on their faces that the can had been opened. That didn't stop me from pressing the matter further though—asking more questions, giving my own knowledgeable interpretation of the scripture. My parents were called before the end of the conversation.

Later I sat in the car, buckled and ready to leave, as my dad spoke with the teachers. He came and got in the car, and leaned in toward me. As was his nature, he gave me the benefit of the doubt.

"So were they picking on you, honey?" he asked. "Tell me what they said." His eyes fixed on mine, and he seemed to be searching for an answer to the question he had likely asked himself every day for the last two years: Was this school right for his daughter? Both of my parents had seen the strain it was putting on my creativity and happiness.

"Well…" I said slowly, "I sort of brought it up." I broke from Dad's gaze and looked down at my chunky blue tights. They were dirty from throwing shot put. Someone's donation.

Dad's voice grew stern. "What did I tell you? Why in the world would you ask those types of questions?" He started the car and we headed home. I wanted to tell him about how bored I was at that school, and how no one liked me. How every day was a practice in isolation—or as close to that as a nine-year-old would have been able to articulate. But I knew that my only other option was public school, so I apologized and went back to the clink the next day. I never instigated another debate in quite such a blatant manner, but regardless, on multiple other occasions going forward I would be resented for my differing faith.

Today the image that comes to mind is of a prisoner whose cell is frequently left open, yet she doesn't escape for fear of what she may find outside. Knowing what I do now, it's almost funny that I would keep subjecting myself to such emotional turmoil to avoid public school because of silly rumors and a fear of the unknown.

Almost.

It seemed I had spent one too many hours staring out that window, because one day I found myself being scorned by the very teacher who had shown me to the coveted seat. "Are you daydreaming? What did I tell you? I'm going to have to give you a demerit, and you're going to move to another cubicle!" I stared up at him as he wrote me up. The last bit of what little happiness I could find in this place was gone.

A few days later I forgot to bring my lunch to school. Mom drove it over, but when she went to open the front door of the schoolhouse she found it locked. Thinking that strange, she knocked.

The teacher walked over to the door and opened it, but only a crack. "I'm sorry, Mrs. Thomas," she said, "but you can't come in through the front door. You need to come in through the back entrance." She looked at my mother disapprovingly, as though this rule were obvious and important enough that she should have known better.

There was a fascinating duality present in my mother. She was as nice a person as you could ever hope to meet. If you wanted to tick her off, you had to do it in *just the right way*. But if you managed to pull it off—if you managed to forge that exact key that would open up the other side of her—she would just about lose her mind. According to legend, as a child she once threw a washing machine down a flight of stairs. This woman had superhuman strength for being a five-foot-tall size-two.

"What do you mean, I can't come in through the front door?" she asked. She was clearly trying to stay calm, but my teacher had already edged her way into that particular part of Mom's brain. The stern, unmoving face squeezed between the door and the jamb provided a good illustration of this concept.

Knowing the sound of a storm a-brewin' when I heard it, I spun in my seat to get a better view of the action.

"We ask that parents use the back entrance during classes," my teacher said. "I'm sorry, but you'll need to go around."

Still calm, but a little less so now: "I'm already here. I'm not going to go all the way around. All you've got to do is move and I can give Elizabeth her lunch, then I'll leave."

The entire affair could have been over by that point. I'll bet Mom could have come in, given me my lunch, had a little of it herself, taught a social studies lesson and been gone. But my teacher was unfazed, and simply wouldn't open the door further. "Those are the rules, Mrs. Thomas."

It was bad enough that my mom had spent two years witnessing her daughter being rejected by a whole group of Christians who should have been building her up. Bad enough that my questions—regardless of their relative lack of tact at times—were met only with hostility. But this seemingly small incident was the straw that broke the camel's back. She busted open the door, shoved past the teacher, grabbed me, and charged out of there.

As she pulled out of the driveway I rolled down the car window and stuck my head out, watching the house recede. Imagine if you would, dear reader, William Wallace from *Braveheart* standing atop a hill, his chest sticking out proudly, his fist raised to the sky, shouting, "FREEDOM!"

Once Mom had made the decision, suddenly I didn't care what waited for me ahead. I would take my chances with the placenta. I was going to public school!

~ three ~

Culture Shock

The elation of escaping the Siberian gulag that was my previous school unfortunately didn't last as long as I'd hoped, and soon the anxiety began to settle over me once more. My bedroom window afforded me a view of the very front of the school, and I opened my curtains on that fateful morning to the sight of excited kids emptying from school buses.

Later, a backpack on my back and fear knotted up in my stomach, I walked with Mom across the street and through the gate into the schoolyard. All around me kids laughed and chatted and ran to their classrooms. I should have been happy to have this fresh start, but all I could think about was how everyone here had been going to school together for years by now; norms had already been established, friendships had already been made… I felt like as much of an outsider as I had at the gulag.

Mom led me to my classroom, and after she managed to pry my hands from hers she kissed me and left me in front of the door. I stood there for a few moments, putting off the actual act of going inside for as long as I could.

Now, considering all of this you might think that I was a reserved and largely unsocial child, but this wasn't the case. Though I don't have quite the penchant my mother did for making friends (there are few in the world who do), I've always been quite outgoing. Before moving to Wilsonville I had no problem interacting with the other kids at my school. But now, after entering a town filled with people who were so strange to me, and after spending two years with a group of kids who rejected me because of my beliefs, the anxiety and the pressure to fit in were mounting. It was more than I could handle.

I racked my brain for any way that I could isolate myself from the situation. The anxiety had my stomach turning over, and mornings were never a great time for me even without it. I always felt sort of gaggy after waking up. Suddenly it came to me: a bathroom stall! At the moment I couldn't think of a place in that entire school that I would rather be! Only a short way down the covered walkway I could see the door to the girls' restroom, which was covered in painted flowers. I made a beeline for it, but it seemed that fate felt I shouldn't be allowed even this small respite from the chaos. A group of boys were roughhousing in the area, and one of them hocked a loogie onto the ground right in front of me.

All bets were off. The sight left me unable to control my bodily functions any longer, and I threw up on the spot, all over the sidewalk. The staff called my mother, and she came and took her humiliated daughter home. It was likely the shortest single day on the school's record.

It's another sort-of-funny story, but its repercussions were anything but. My young mind was unable to identify the source of its anxiety, so in order to protect itself from the unfathomable dangers (and/or loogies) that lurked around every corner on those grounds, it developed an irrational fear of going to school. Each morning after the first one my parents had to fight with me to make me go. At the forefront of my mind was the fear of throwing up again, which fed into my anxiety, which then of course just strengthened the urge to throw up. This pattern of thought followed me through my first several years at that school. Fear was at the base of all my decisions. And since I had no confidence and was afraid of what awaited me each and every day, the only possible way to cope was to hide—often in my room, with my TV and a bowl of peanut butter covered in powdered sugar (that is, when I could sneak the bowl past my mom).

The hope that I would eventually acclimate to this strange environment faded a little with each year. The voice in my head reminding me that I was different from the people around me never went away; in fact, it seemed to grow stronger over time. Every day at school was a reminder of how much I didn't belong there—how much my upbringing differed from the culture surrounding me. So much of this was only in my mind—most of the kids and teachers were perfectly welcoming—but that hardly mattered. The complete and utter lack of Christian peers was something I couldn't seem to get used to. I stood out from the crowd in that respect, and I knew it.

One afternoon in the fifth grade our teacher, Mrs. Weed (believe me, the irony of the name is not lost on me), taught the class about drugs.

She told a story about a friend's son, who couldn't be in the FBI because he had smoked pot in high school. She told us that they could test a piece of your hair and know what drugs you had taken.

"I would like you to raise your hand if you've never seen a pot plant before," she said. The class of twenty students was silent as she scanned the room. Likely daydreaming about what I was going to watch when I got home, I paid little attention to the rest of the class and raised my hand honestly like a good little church mouse. It was a moment before I came to and realized that my hand was the only one in the air.

Mrs. Weed placed a picture of a pot plant on my desk and I looked down at it, not exactly knowing what to think. It might as well have been a unicorn. An elf. Bigfoot. Some mythical creature that I knew basically nothing about. After examining it I forced a smile and handed it back to her. Then Mrs. Weed gave the little church mouse one last opportunity to feel at least a little normal and asked the class once more if any of them hadn't yet seen a pot plant.

You can guess how many hands went up. A big fat zero.

A little trivia on the place I grew up: Two thirds of the economy in the tri-county area is directly related to the cultivation of marijuana. Back in the 80's and 90's it was still highly illegal, and permits for the growing of medical marijuana simply didn't exist yet. The majority of the people in our community either worked at the small timber mill or grew pot. Some were teachers, or owned small businesses, but most fell into those first two camps.

The town held such a small population, yet still a decently diverse one. Plenty of white people, a few black families, a number of Mexicans, and a large Native American population, the majority of which lived on a reservation. If you were forced to lump all of the residents of Wilsonville into two primary groups you could call them the hippies and the rednecks. Hippies that grew pot, rednecks that cut timber, hippies that protested the cutting of timber, rednecks that smoked pot but hated the hippies, Native Americans that grew pot *and* cut timber, and the few that simply lived in the middle of it all.

I know, I know, I'm stereotyping and mixing ethnicities with subculture. But believe me when I say I use "hippy" and "redneck" in a purely endearing way, and most residents of the town themselves would probably even say that this was an accurate assessment. In fact, since Mom and Dad's families originated from the South, we fit somewhat comfortably into the redneck category.

Religious differences played a large part in my feelings of isolation, but there was more to it than that. Just as it was at the heart of our community, pot was also at the heart of what made me and my family different from the rest of the town. It was and still is a part of the culture of Wilsonville, but it's also so much more; sometimes it seems it *is* the culture. There are many who grow, and many who don't. There are some who use it casually, and there are those who worship it with everything inside them—exalt it like a god. But it permeates everything, exists as an entity all its own, and is as much a part of Wilsonville's commerce as the single grocery store.

All of that was of course more than I knew at the time, but the vague sense of it was enough to set me apart. My parents on the other hand seemed to have an uncanny knack for taking everything in stride, and for overlooking these stark differences. From the beginning their mission was to love anyone and everyone they met, regardless of what they smoked or believed. And one of the biggest ways they loved was through their generosity.

four

Giving

"I was wondering if I could get some money. I'm just passing through town and I've hit hard times." The voice at the door had what I would later come to know as the unmistakable quality of a transient person: friendly but startling in its volume; slightly slurred as though from alcohol, or brain damage, or a little of both; still holding onto the 70's way of speech, as though his mind remained back at the war from which he never fully recovered. I peeked around the corner and saw him at the door, speaking loudly despite Mom standing right in front of him. He wore camo pants and a tattered jacket, and had several days' growth on his face.

He waited patiently as Mom went to speak with Dad, and after a short exchange Dad went to the door. "Hi there," he said with a smile. "We don't have any money that we can give you right now, but we can give you a meal. Can we make you a sandwich?" The man graciously accepted and waited on the porch as my parents made him lunch. Dad was visibly disappointed that he couldn't do more.

Through the window beside the front door I watched as he brought out the lunch and sat with the man while he ate. The man was very grateful, and gave Dad a hug when he brought it out. As he was taking the last few bites of his sandwich he told my dad: "You know your house is marked, right?"

Dad looked confused. "Marked?" he asked.

"Yeah, we mark places that are willing to help us. I can't tell you how, but you're marked. Thank you for your kindness, brother." And with that, he left.

The next day Dad went under the house to see if he could find the source of the noises he had heard the previous night. Our house was built on a hill and sat on a raised wooden foundation, so there was an expanse of dirt underneath (as well as about a jillion potato bugs), including one basement-like area with a door on the side of the house. Expecting to find a skunk or an opossum, he instead found trash and other evidence that the man in the camo pants had slept there the night before. Further inspection revealed that many other transients had been sleeping down there as well. He cleaned up the mess and bought a padlock for the door. He never got on anyone's case about it, not even once. In fact on more than one occasion he allowed people to sleep in the shed behind the church, though that was fairly rare.

Transients coming right up to our door to ask for food and money was a regular part of life growing up (and I only truly appreciated in later years how unusual that was). The highway went right through town and the church was visible from it, so we were a bit of a hot spot. It was understood in our household that they could come at any time, and it was a rare occasion when one of them left empty-handed, if it ever happened at all. Many of these people were war vets that felt discarded by society. And each one of them left with a sandwich and a little bag of chips. Just as it's important to know who my parents were in order to know who I am, it's important to know just how generous they were, even though they never had much extra to give.

After a while in Wilsonville I did manage to make friends, and they were always surprised to witness this generosity in action. One memory stands out in particular. One day my friend Krystal came over and we were playing on the massive stump that sat in the middle of our yard. The rotten old pine tree had been felled shortly before we moved in, leaving us with a great big stump about four feet wide (and with enough firewood to last several winters). We were playing on this, no doubt affixing a large amount of sap permanently to our shoes, when a van pulled up to our yard. A young woman got out, and we could see four kids sitting inside.

"Hi," the woman said nervously, "I'm wondering if anyone here can help my family."

Seeing someone in need, I acted. And by *acted*, I mean *ran inside and got my mom*. It was all a part of my training, and I was quite good at it.

Mom came out and greeted the woman. She smiled and shook Mom's hands, but soon there were tears in her eyes. "I'm so sorry to bother you, but I've run out of gas, and we still have two hours to make it to our house."

Mom nodded understandingly and told her they would see if they could work something out. She went back inside, and a few moments later returned with Dad.

My father could be a little intimidating because of his looks. He was a large man, at over three hundred pounds, and much of the already very subtle expressions of his face were lost behind the weight and his beard. One might look at him and see a grumpy guy, but the truth was that he was a tender and patient man. His seemingly stern looks were only due to the discomfort he felt in his own skin. Perhaps sensing that the woman was slightly intimidated by his presence, he waved Krystal and me over.

"Girls," he said brightly, "how about you go get my keys so we can help this lady get some gas!" We ran inside and grabbed the keys, and soon we were piled into our brown Plymouth Caravelle.

And it might be beside the point, but I remember that car with a good amount of fondness; my friend no doubt had a good laugh when a pre-recorded voice came from the car to tell us: "A door is ajar." As a Star Trek fan and tech junkie, my dad took a lot of pride in having a talking car—the last remnant of financial bliss from his days at HP. He would later earn the nickname "Pastor Gadget."

Our destination was the gas station two blocks down the road. Yes, we drove, despite it being visible from our house. In case you couldn't tell, we weren't the most active family. Dad put gas in the lady's car—enough to get her home and then some. She thanked him profusely and drove away, then Dad grabbed some soda for dinner and we headed home. In my room, eating the candy we'd likely begged for, Krystal seemed to be confused.

"Did your parents know that lady?" she asked.

"No," I said casually.

"Then why did they buy her gas?"

"Because that's my parents' job. To help people." And with that I popped a Starburst into my mouth, and soon we went and had dinner. My friends were always very eager to come to my house so they could score some of the various fried and/or cheese-filled foods that were banned in their own homes, and this meal didn't disappoint: lavish amounts of Velveeta cheese melted in a pot with canned tomatoes and onions and poured over fried corn tortillas stuffed with ground beef. Krystal ate a hearty helping and proceeded to flee to the bathroom and vomit. Poor, poor organic child…

When I told Krystal that helping others was my parents' job I wasn't trying to play it cool or anything; it truly was a normal part of everyday life for us. They were equipped with a kindness that sometimes shocked people, and that I've even struggled to emulate throughout my own life, if I'm being honest. In fact, you could easily say they were generous to a fault, often failing to establish boundaries when they were needed. My dad would tell you about the time he let someone he barely knew borrow his other (non-verbal) car, only to find it crashed and abandoned a few towns over.

It was incredible that they were able to give when the budget was so tight, but even more so when that budget was tightened further by an unexpected but welcome new guest.

With the way churchgoers go about a Sunday afternoon, you would think that scrolled on Moses' stone tablet, right under the fourth Commandment, was an extra line. It would read something like, "Remember the Sabbath, and keep it holy…and eat dinner during lunchtime, and eat way too much."

Whether an actual commandment or not, we certainly did remember that particular part of the Sabbath, and we kept it very holy. On one Sunday when I was eight, hoping to slip into the standard post-dinner coma with the sound of lawnmowers buzzing in the distance like lazy bees, I plunked down onto my bed and reached for the remote. (And despite the large dinner I'd just had, I nevertheless clutched a bowl of peanut butter with powdered sugar.) But before I could turn on the TV, my mom walked into the room.

Her eyes were filled with news. "Guess what?" she asked. At the moment I had a huge spoonful of obesity in my mouth, so she blurted it out before I could guess: "You're going to be a big sister!" She beamed at me and rubbed her belly.

It took a few moments before my mind could really grasp what she was saying. Years of praying every night before bed had finally paid off! The daily ritual of the Only Child would change. Tears filled my eyes even as peanut butter still filled my mouth.

She had managed to conceive her second baby despite the doctors' insistence that it was impossible, but the pregnancy was hard on her; she spent most of it confined to her bed. Soon however, Jackie Vandall Thomas III (named so after our father and his father before him) was born. And having a baby brother that was two weeks shy of nine years younger than me—old enough to carry, change, feed, burp, and cuddle as necessary—was like owning a living doll.

Our little house only had two bedrooms, so for the first several years of his life Jackie slept on a bed in the living room. And in those early years he never slept through the night, and screamed like crazy when he was upset, which was often. Mom referred to it as his "Dr. Jekyll and Mr. Hyde personality." We never knew when Mr. Hyde would arrive, but when he did, you could hear it across the street. It wasn't until later that we discovered his food allergy—a sensitivity to sugar and red food dye. Once cookies and Jell-O and other sugary foods were taken out of the equation he slept through the night and his behavior mellowed. Against just about everyone's expectations, he turned out to be a very loveable and often quiet child. Dr. Jekyll had, very fortunately, won out in the end.

This addition to the family was yet another strain on our finances, but no matter how hard things got it seemed that there was always enough. Continuing the legacy of provision, our family would often receive aid ourselves when we most needed it and least expected it. Multiple times we were "adopted" around Christmas time by other larger churches in California; they would invite us to stay with them, and the congregation would give us presents and a lot of food. Our shelves would be packed with cans when we were done, many of which we were able to give to the transients, thus perpetuating the cycle of giving.

But perhaps more amazingly, we received a huge amount of support from the community. Every once in a while the ladies in the church would hold a bake sale over at the post office (which was a stone's throw away). I have distinct memories of those days:

I would sit behind the table with Katherine, one of Mom's best friends. Even from a young age I was very close with her, and she's always been one of the sweetest and most wise women of God I've known. Her house was like a second home, and I would even go over there for sleepovers (well, at least I would try to sleepover, but then almost always buckle under my anxiety and have Mom come pick me up).

We would sell to the other members of the church, staff from the school, the people picking up their mail and going about their day. Then, every once in a while, one of a great number of beat-up trucks would rumble its way into the parking lot. A man or a woman would get out and come up to the table, smiling. They would pull a great big wad of cash out of their pocket and often hugely overpay for one of the treats displayed there.

I mentioned how much of the town's population grew pot, and it was these people that most loved to pop up whenever there was a bake sale or yard sale or any other fundraising event. These weren't drug lords living in fancy mansions and driving Hummers or anything like that; they were regular folks who worked hard in the garden every day in order to support their families. Small business owners who took joy in producing something from the land. They paid with cash because cash was all they dealt with. They drove beat up cars and lived in modest houses, and always made it a point to give to the community in any way they could. My parents didn't agree with everything they did, but always showed them nothing but friendliness and the utmost respect. These people in turn respected and admired my parents, despite their differing beliefs. The result was an amazing sense of community that would hugely impact my view of the world and how I came to interact with people from different backgrounds.

There were many who appreciated what my parents did, but Mom and Dad would do everything in their power to help even those who weren't fully able to give their appreciation. I remember one such person very vividly…

~ five ~

A Sandwich for Barney

Sometimes it seemed the phone was surgically attached to my mom's head. This particular phone call however didn't bring a smile to her face as most did. After a while of listening and nodding she only said, "Okay Barney, we'll be right there," and hung up the phone.

I was sitting on the couch reading something, and Mom walked by me on her way to grab her jacket and keys. "Elizabeth, I need you to come with me," she said. "Barney's out of bread, and he's having one of his episodes." She gave a sigh of concern as she plucked her keys from the holder. I put on my own jacket and shoes and we headed out to our second car, a red, stick-shift 1980's Datsun.

I loved that car. Hopping in with my mom in the driver's seat would always give me a tiny pang of guilt though, because it and I had more of a history than my parents realized. Only a few months earlier when they were out of town for the night I had asked my babysitter casually if I could take the car out for a drive, and had actually gotten a plain old *yes*.

Little did Mom and Dad know that their sweet little middle-schooler had been joyriding around the neighborhood at midnight, driving through people's yards and nearly taking out mailboxes as her friends laughed hysterically from the back seat. They never would find out about it, either.

Today was no joyride however, and after picking up some bread we headed to Barney's house. Leading up to the visit was never pleasant, because you never knew how Barney was going to be acting when you got there. He was never violent, but that didn't make him much less unnerving, particularly to a young girl. We pulled off the road and climbed the incredibly steep driveway, which reminded me of the streets in San Francisco. We parked and approached the house, and as always the dark windows and the junk piled on the porch made the place feel less-than-welcoming. When we reached the door Mom used the doorknocker that looked like an owl on a bad acid trip. It stared at us with its crazy jewel eyes as she hit the ring in its talons against the wood three times.

The door immediately opened a crack, stopping on the chain, and one bloodshot eye stared out at us from the dark of the house. "Friend or foe?" Barney asked without a hint of humor.

"Friend, Barney." My mom's voice was calm and patient, much as though she were talking to a child. "It's Ruth and Elizabeth. We've got your bread. Please open up." He unlatched the chain and opened the door, and we walked in.

Barney, a Vietnam vet and schizophrenic, loved his little cave, and there were periods of time when he wouldn't step foot into the light of day for weeks (or longer if he had been skipping his medication). Dad had met him some years back when the man was walking into town. It was ninety degrees outside and Barney was severely dehydrated, so Dad offered to give him a lift. Since then he had made sure to check in on Barney every once in a while and make sure he made his doctor's appointments.

Like many of the people my parents attended to and kept an eye on, Barney was a hoarder, and as such, his house was filled with junk. With the curtains drawn and much of the space taken up by God-knew-what-all, the place felt a little claustrophobic. I followed Mom meekly to the kitchen and awkwardly stood in the archway.

Mom went through the cabinets, looking for the right condiments. "Tuna fish or chicken salad today?" she called.

At that Barney came into the kitchen, walked right up to me, and put his face three inches from mine. I held my breath as he regarded me, without a clue as to what might be going through his head. Then he blurted out, "Chicken!" and walked off. Despite my best efforts the assault breached my nostrils. His breath smelled like cigars and weed.

My mom watched him eat the sandwich, and when he was just about finished she rose to leave. She knew he was more likely to take his meds on a full stomach.

"Please take your pills, Barney," she said. "We want you to sleep well and have good dreams. Call us tomorrow when you wake up."

"They can't control my mind!" he barked in his usual talk-shout. "They never will! They can watch me all they want, but I won't be poisoned!" I remember being surprised by how well he managed to keep his food in his mouth despite the loud protest. I suppose he'd had a lot of practice.

We said goodbye and left. He was still ranting to himself about how he wouldn't take his medication while we were closing the front door, but Mom knew that after the visit and the lunch he would eventually do it. Somehow it always seemed to do the trick.

We got into the Datsun and Mom turned the key. Nothing happened.

"Shoot, not again!" Mom frowned down at the ignition. "We're going to have to roll start it." She instructed me to get out and push from the front of the car until we hit the steeper part of the driveway, while she sat with one leg out the door. We got it rolling and Mom tried to pop the clutch, but still it wouldn't start. Now she was close to the road and was forced to stop and try to come up with a new plan. She put the car in park and started to get out, but the brake slipped. The car rolled down the remainder of the hill and into the road, and Mom, panicking, could only run backwards while the door pushed her along with it. Now the car raced toward the rise on the other side of the street. All of this happened so fast, in the space of a few seconds, and there was no time for me to respond. The best I could manage was to shout, "Mom! It's going to hit!" And just as the words finished coming out of my mouth the rear end of the car struck the rise. Mom just barely managed to get out of the way of the door and her back crashed onto the weedy earth.

My heart pounding, I ran down the hill and over to Mom, who was picking herself up and dusting off her pants. "I'm okay," she assured me, "just a few scrapes. Get in the car so you don't get hit."

We climbed into the car and it started in one try. We were quiet for most of the drive home. When we were nearly there she muttered, "I should have called your father. That was stupid." She pulled back her sleeve and looked down at the scrape on her arm. I sat silently as she pulled into our driveway, the image of the rolling car and of her crashing into the rise playing through my mind in a loop. It was the first time I had ever feared losing my mother, and it seemed that all at once the very concept of death had become much more real. It had showed up suddenly and rudely, like an unwanted guest. Mom unbuckled her seatbelt and was about to open her door when I spoke.

"Mom, do you think you'll live a long life?"

The bluntness of the question gave her pause, and she stopped what she was doing and looked at me. She studied my face for a moment, and then said, "I was ten when my mother died. I've asked the Lord to give me a long life so that I can see you grow up, like my mother never got to." She gave me a reassuring smile, and we went inside.

~ six ~

My Date with Bigfoot

Naive. Untouched. Pure. Innocent. These are some of the words I would use to describe my twelve-year-old self before one particular kid started coming over after school. But once she came, things took a very different turn.

Mom made some extra money by watching kids after school for parents who had to work late. Our home was obviously a perfect fit because of its location—a location that was convenient in many ways, but pretty inconvenient whenever I wanted to take one of my many "sick" days. One of the kids Mom watched was April, and from the beginning she and I had a love-hate relationship. I could have been wrong, but it felt like her mission in life was to change me.

There was a lot of space to roam and explore in Wilsonville, and with our house in the middle of town all we had to do was pick a direction and start walking. Woods, empty fields, a few cows and horses, and old houses filled the block. A sleepy town for the most part, and safe to explore. One day we were walking around, and I was trailing behind April, who was now speeding up. I remember pulling at my shirt, which was too tight around the waist. This was a constant problem, and in April's presence I felt particularly self-conscious about it.

One good thing about living so far away from anything was that all the other kids at the public school wore clothes that were just as junky as mine. The disadvantage to being a kid that was both poor *and* fat however, was that not only were my clothes old but they usually didn't fit right and they weren't age-appropriate. In the eighties and early nineties kids' plus-size sections in department stores were virtually non-existent, which meant my options were limited. Dress for success for less in a floral grandmother dress.

"Come on, Liz, keep up!" she shouted back at me. "I want to show you something!" She stopped in the driveway of one of her relatives' homes and I finally caught up. We walked up to the house, April grabbed a key from under the doormat, and we let ourselves in.

She flicked on the lights with a wicked grin on her face. "They're gone for a week! We can hang out here as much as we want!" She looked to see my reaction and caught the fear in my eyes. "Relax," she said. "Nobody's going to know we're here. And if someone does ask, I'll just tell them we were watering the plants." With a foolproof plan in place, I did begin to relax. We headed for the kitchen.

Opening the fridge, I spotted a ton of chocolate in the meat drawer. "Do you think it's okay if I have some?" I asked. My eyes glistened with excitement.

"Liz, what have I told you about your weight?" she answered with an eye roll. "You can't eat candy if you're trying to lose weight."

Close to tears, I hid my face and sat down at the kitchen table. Rejection sat with me.

This was at the crux of our relationship. April had a strong desire to achieve a certain body image, and she projected this desire onto me. She was always on a low-fat diet and constantly exercising, and the need for male approval even at such a young age seemed to dominate her life. Since she couldn't fully control her own life, it felt like I became her project. She even went as far as making me posters of supermodels and hanging them on my wall in order to motivate me not to eat. And amid all this I clung to her, so badly wanting friends. It was only one of many situations to follow wherein I would trade away my power for acceptance. I don't blame her in any way—we were both just being insecure kids—but my relationship with her definitely had a great impact on me, and in more ways than one.

"Come here and help me," April said. "I have something way better than candy." She pulled a chair up to the fridge, climbed on top of it, and opened a small cupboard. She pulled out something large and clear and handed it down to me. In my hands I held a big bottle of vodka.

And just like in a classic after-school special, I drank to be loved. We sat on the couch, sipping from the bottle, and I had my first experience with the numbing qualities of intoxication. After a few drinks, however, my bladder felt as though it was going to explode, so I tried to compose myself as I stumbled to the bathroom. I sat on the commode and looked down at the magazines on the floor. I didn't find recipes for chocolate cookies or methods for successfully cleaning my garage in this pile...

This was porn. A great big pile of porn, just sitting there, plain as day, no big deal. This was another mythical creature. It was like Bigfoot had just walked by the window.

We stayed there until we sobered up. I stole the chocolate out of the fridge while April was puking in the bathroom. How my parents didn't smell it on us when we got back to my house, I'll never know. Neither of them ever drank; Mom had a sip of wine once and hated it, and when Dad was young he once went to take a drink of beer when his grandfather smacked him from behind; he took it as a sign from God and never touched alcohol again. Naive and wanting to believe that their little girl could do no wrong, they missed the first sign. They would miss many signs in the future.

seven

Mom's Book

Another in a long line of Sunday afternoons was drifting by. Mom visited with a few of her church friends while Dad tidied up the sanctuary. In a congregation of thirty people Dad wasn't just the pastor, but the janitor, worship leader, counselor, accountant, and so on.

Little Jackie whizzed by me as we walked back to the house to eat lunch. "Come on, Sissy! Let's watch TV in my room!" His blonde hair, which contained within it the most stubborn cowlick you've ever laid eyes on, bounced in the sun as he ran. Four years old and adorable, though even as a young teenager I felt he was growing up fast.

I caught him right before he could open the door, hoisted him up, and planted a kiss on his cheek big enough to make him squirm. Then we went inside and flopped down onto his bed. By now Dad had relocated his home office to the church and given Jackie the dining area off of the kitchen as his first almost-real room (though at that point it still had no door to speak of).

After we watched puppets dance around for a bit, Mom came in the house and grabbed the phone. "Honey, can you get me all the dishes in the living room so I can clean up and cook?" she asked. Then she stuck the phone to her ear and was off. She loved to talk as she cooked. Her tiny frame danced around the kitchen as she chatted and laughed with her friend. "A stranger's just a friend you haven't met" was an expression my Mom took to heart, and as a one hundred percent extrovert she thrived on relationships.

I headed to the living room and gathered up the dishes, most of which were mine. I was notorious for drinking half a cup and leaving it before starting another one. Perhaps I was unconsciously channeling the little girl from the movie *Signs*, preparing against an alien invasion.

As I picked up the last of the dishes from the coffee table, a book caught my eye. It sat next to a stack of the usual cheesy Christian romance novels that my mom was fond of, so I very nearly ignored it. You know the type I'm talking about; a clean romance about a woman in pioneer days, living a simple life and overcoming obstacles with the love of a great big hunk of a man—or a woman in the days of one of the great wars, waiting for a far-off love to manifest or for a great big hunk of a man to come home safely. Snoozeball. You can bet that Dad never missed an opportunity to tease her about them.

I was about to take the stack of cups and plates to the kitchen, but at the last possible second I paused and glanced at the cover of this book:

Bible Devotions for Overcoming Sexual Abuse.

Books on counseling subjects weren't uncommon in our home. Dad spent many hours with people in the church who were overcoming addictions and other hardships. But this book stood out to me.

I walked into the kitchen, where Mom's phone conversation had apparently ended early. She stood at the sink with her back to me, doing a few dishes. Before taking my stack to the sink I asked, "Mom, why is there a book about sexual abuse on the coffee table?"

She didn't turn to me; she only kept her eyes on the sink. After a moment she said, "It's my book," and left it at that.

I brought over the dishes and dropped them into the soapy water. I glanced at her face, and I saw shame there. Without pressing for more information I walked to my room and closed the door. I lay on my bed, not knowing exactly what to think.

After a few minutes I heard the slam of the screen door and the familiar, joking call of "Where's my dinner, woman?" I couldn't hear what Dad said next, but I could hear the lightheartedness leave his voice as he exchanged a few words with Mom. After a moment of silence I crept up to my door and opened it a crack. Both of them were standing with their backs to me now, Dad's arm around Mom and her head on his shoulder. Dad gave her shoulder a squeeze and began to turn, so I shut the door and ran back to my bed, hastily picking up a magazine and pretending to read as I heard the approaching footsteps. He knocked softly on my door and walked in with a concerned look on his face. Happiness wasn't always clearly visible on his face, as I mentioned before, but concern somehow had a way of showing through.

"Hi dear," he said. "I just wanted to tell you your song today in church was really nice. I know that the Lord really loved to hear it."

His eyes met mine, and I started to cry. I felt like I had done something wrong, and I didn't understand what was going on. Probably sensing this, Dad sat down beside me on the bed and looked closer into my eyes. He took the magazine from my hands and put it down, and being the incredible listener that he was, let me start. "Is there something you want to talk about?" he asked.

I tried to hold back my confused, angry tears. "Why is Mom reading that book?"

Dad obviously knew the question was coming, but still took a moment to answer. Many believe that in a proper Christian home, these things are simply not talked about. That was the way my parents were raised, as were their parents before them. But Dad answered anyway.

"Your mother was sexually abused by her father, and later by a pastor she trusted." Now he was looking down at the floor, weighing his words carefully, obviously uncomfortable with the subject matter but wanting to be as truthful as possible. He'd always been an excellent communicator. "That's why it's hard for her to talk about sex," he continued. "It's the first time she's wanted to see someone about it and get help. She's dealing with a lot. I understand that it's probably very confusing for you."

Confusing was an understatement. Algebra was confusing. Squarely hitting a volleyball only to have it fly off and hit a spectator was confusing. Mom not being able to figure out how to set the cruise control on the car was confusing. This was not just confusing. This was the end of the safe, impenetrable home I'd grown up in. In the span of a few minutes everything I had thought I'd known about God and our family had crumbled around me. The God I was taught about would always keep us safe from pain if we did what He asked. Mom had done everything He asked and then some, and in return had been robbed.

After our talk Dad left, and we all continued living our normal lives. Well, for Mom and Dad at least everything might have seemed normal, but yet another change had taken place in my mind, and a floodgate of thoughts and realizations had been opened. The more I thought about things, the more it made sense as to why all of my friends were able to talk openly about sex with their parents, but my mom was extremely uncomfortable with the subject. I had always assumed that it was just the difference between a Christian and a non-Christian family.

In fact, I recalled with renewed clarity the day Mom and I were at a Christian bookstore and I saw a book on teaching kids about sex. I had picked it up and told Mom, "I think you need to buy this for me." She bought it without question and never spoke of it again.

Because of my parents' traditional upbringings and Mom's abuse, the subject of sex always came with undertones of shame; that picture had become clearer to me, as unpleasant as it was. And even though finding out about Mom's issues filled in some of the missing pieces of her journey in my mind, it colored my perception of who I was and would continue to do so as I later began to identify my own sexuality. The seeds of change were growing rapidly.

～ eight ～

Strawberry Milkshake

I was awake long before my alarm clock went off. By the time it did I couldn't even tell how long I'd been staring at the ceiling. I got up, showered, and dressed, feeling the knot of dread in my stomach grow tighter with each passing minute. By eight o'clock both my heartbeat and my breathing were coming fast. I was queasy, as I'd known I would be.

As I often did during my school career thus far, I found myself standing in front of Mom as she drank her morning coffee on the couch. I gave a well-rehearsed grimace and grabbed my stomach.

"Mom, I really don't feel good. I think I'm going to throw up." I knew it was lame, but I was that desperate.

She looked up at me. "You're going, Elizabeth," she said simply.

I knew that if I pushed hard enough she would eventually give. I'd even convinced my dad to homeschool me for a big portion of middle school because of my irrational fears. And this was a new school with a whole new set of fears. High school might as well have been a scary foreign country where no one speaks your language and everyone yells and you're forced to work in a mine and sleep on garbage. If there was a time to fight going to school, it was now.

"But I'm seriously sick!" I said, putting a little extra pain in my face and nausea in my voice. "If I go now I'll probably throw up in the hallway before I even get to class!"

"*You're going*," she repeated, and the sternness in her voice took me by surprise. "You're going to have to face this. You can't hide at home forever." And that was the last she said on the matter.

So I went to school, but I was very surprised to find that it wasn't as bad as I'd feared. The kids were older, the work was harder, the teachers were very eclectic and it was bigger (compared to our middle school, which was a handful of classrooms surrounding a small quad area), but it came with a certain feeling of freedom that I found comforting. ("We're allowed to walk into town on our lunch break and buy greasy burgers *every day*? Sign me up!") Plus I had made a few friends in middle school, and they were all there with me. My true saving grace however, came after the first day was over.

I played volleyball in middle school and had really loved playing the game and being part of a team. When tryouts took place in the high school gym I very nearly chickened out, but mustered up the courage and made the team. This was an important event for me, and I found that the stress of school was lessened considerably when I focused on the sport. Even coming in at sixty pounds overweight I played well, usually as a starting string. Travelling with the team gave me great opportunities to face my fears, despite being the subject of the usual ridicule. Every single season I feared that the new uniform wouldn't fit me. Guys from opposing towns would laugh and toss insults at me as I walked by. It was typical high school bullying, but that didn't make it any less painful. I was blessed, however, to have good friends who supported me, and a community that would cheer me on at every home game. For the first time in my life I found a little confidence rising up inside me.

And with that confidence came a renewed desire—one that had been with me since middle school but was now stronger than ever: I desperately wanted a boyfriend.

Naturally all of my friends were rotating through guys—sometimes it seemed like one a week. The problem was that in a school of one hundred twenty-five, it was slim pickings. Not understanding why no one was seeking me out, I decided to take matters into my own hands.

I had it bad for a guy named Seth, who was a class ahead of me. I wrote him a long letter confessing my attraction. It may or may not have ended with *yes* and *no* checkboxes, though I'm at least confident that I was conservative in my use of the term "like-like." I told him about all of his qualities that I loved: his kindness, his flair for the dramatic, his tendency to mostly hang around girls, the feminine manner in which he spoke… Yeah, I was clueless, to say the least. Fortunately, he let me down gently.

After that day with April I had continued to drink on a regular basis. It's the social drug after all, and at any gathering where no parents were present, there was sure to be booze. Things *really* shifted one night at a party…

I wanted more than anything to fit in at school, but there was still a part of me that longed for my days in Mountain View, when I had Christian friends and there was no conflict between my religion and my social life. So when I befriended a couple of girls from a nearby church, I thought things might be on track again. One day Mom and Dad went on an overnight trip with Jackie, so with the house to myself I decided to throw a party. I invited the girls over and they brought a few of their friends. The first thing they all did when they arrived was break out the weed.

That night I smoked pot for the first time, and for the first time in my life I felt my anxiety just fall away into nothing. Drinking was fun, but this numbed me to my core and allowed me to just forget about my pain and my worries. While I was high I could just check out, and it was an immense relief.

The girls ended up convincing me to invite more people, and eventually the whole thing escalated into a crazy party that refused to end until the next morning and left the house trashed. I spent hours cleaning up with one of my friends and miraculously Mom and Dad never found out about it; Mom only thanked me for dusting her shelf of fancy porcelain bells, which I had done during my meticulous sweep. Overall, the night had been an awful experience and I didn't hang out with those two girls much after that, but they had introduced me to a new method of escape.

After that night, smoking was a regular part of my life, along with drinking. I grew to crave and depend on the numbing quality of these substances, and I partook any time I wasn't at home or school. With these new band-aids in place I continued to forge my way through high school and into more friendships.

Reaching the legal driving age did even more to bolster my confidence, and when I got my permit I was out of my mind with excitement. On my sixteenth birthday my grandparents surprised me with a little Plymouth hatchback—my grandparents…who lived in Oklahoma. I was extremely thankful for the gift, but waiting *six months* before they hitched it to their mobile home and came to visit was pure torture. If you've ever been a kid you'll remember how six months felt more like four and a half years. The day it arrived though, I felt as though my wings had sprouted.

One of my favorite activities in those early days was driving twenty-five minutes down the highway to the nearest fast food drive-through. One Saturday I scraped together enough change for a quarter-pounder with cheese and a strawberry milkshake. I drove home through the winding roads, relishing both the drive and my fries, when a car swerved into my lane and forced me off the road.

I slammed into the exact beginning of a guard rail; it just barely kept me from going over the steep embankment and my seatbelt kept me from flying through the windshield. When the horrific moment was over I sat there, and red liquid was oozing down my face. "Oh my gosh," I said distantly, "my head is bleeding." Panicking, I ran my hands over my body to check for further injuries, and noticed that the same liquid was soaking my pants.

I licked some of the ooze from my finger. Strawberry. I looked over and saw the empty milkshake cup on the seat next to me.

Relieved but still shaking, I got out of the car. The lady who had caused the accident was shaking as well, and stayed with me until the ambulance pulled up.

The doors flung open and out jumped none other than Seth, who was interning with the EMT program. I may have survived the crash, but my life was officially over. Emphasizing each syllable hugely and dramatically with his arms he shouted as he ran over to me: "*Oh-my-GOD*, Liz! Are you okay?!"

Strawberry gunk dripped down my face as my shaken and hormone-addled brain imagined that for some reason the paramedics would have to cut my clothes off to look for injuries when I got into the ambulance. You know, like in the movies! Seth was going to see me *naked*! I nearly drowned in the horror of it.

Thankfully he took my pulse and looked at some of my scratches and that was it. I opted out of the ambulance ride when a neighbor who had been passing by offered to take me to the hospital. (Did I mention it was a small town?) Poor Dad was informed that I had been in a wreck and was on my way to the hospital, though he didn't know much beyond that. My totaled car was being towed back to town and he had to pass it on his way to see me. Fortunately all he found when he arrived were a few scratches, one mother of a bruise on my boob, and a wounded ego.

When it was all said and done the following week, my mom forced me behind the wheel so I wouldn't develop a fear of driving. It was another one of the few times she gave me a direct order, and again I'm glad she did it.

Suffice it to say, after that day I gave up my pursuit of Mr. Seth.

nine

Crossroads

Taking up volleyball gave me a new sense of confidence, and getting my license gave me the freedom I'd desired for so many years, but sometimes one's skin can only grow so thick. The insecurities that had plagued me since moving to Wilsonville had continued to grow over the years. I had a few friends, and I'll always be grateful for their presence during this period, but even after so much time in the Wilsonville school district, I still carried with me a spirit of rejection.

I might not have ever explicitly admitted all this to myself, and I might not even have quite understood it at the time, but at least on a subconscious level it seemed that there were two sources of this rejection. One of them was my weight. This was a struggle largely because of its cyclical nature: I felt I was rejected because of my weight, which made me take comfort in food, which added to the weight problem, which left me feeling rejected, etc. Then throw in the fact that we had little money and even less knowledge about nutrition. I didn't feel strong enough to take control of that issue, so I focused on what I *perceived* as the second source of rejection: the dichotomy between my family's Christian faith and the atheism/pseudo-spiritual agnosticism of most of the community.

The crack in my faith that had appeared when I found Mom's book had also been widening over the years, and by my junior year of high school this became an area that I felt I actually had some control over. My new strategy in my ongoing fight for acceptance was to completely detach from my parents.

Because of my anxiety problems I was once more back at home doing independent study, but despite that, I did all I could to separate from the traditions of my family. By now I had been using drugs and alcohol for several years, yet because of my parents' naivety when it came to that sort of stuff my usage still remained hidden.

Up until high school we only had access to four TV channels, and we were all ecstatic when satellite TV was made available in our area. I'd always had a TV in my room growing up, so now I had a whole new world of stuff to watch. I was surprised to find that soft porn was readily available late at night. I watched whenever I could, and soon I looked to it as another form of escape along with drugs and alcohol. Because of the general fear of talking about sex in our house, I never even dreamed of bringing it up with my parents. It just became yet another layer of shame to remain hidden and fester year after year.

My ultimate goal in life was now to find refuge from the pain, and to me that also meant running away from anything having to do with the Church. The rules of my parents' religion no longer felt like they were keeping me safe; now they were caging me in.

Growing up I had constantly witnessed what I perceived as a lack of strength from my mom, so I began searching for other sources of feminine strength. From what I could tell through stories, her own mother had given up her voice and had simply accepted that she was nothing. Because of this and because of the abuse, my mom often battled with her own self-worth. She struggled with the lie that she was unintelligent. She was friendly, safe, and kind to a fault, so people tended to love her right off the bat; because of this and her willingness to back down in a conflict however, they sometimes walked all over her as well. To her, ministry meant that you gave everything and then some, and the exploitation this could invite perpetuated her feelings of worthlessness.

Generations of women in my family had given away their power, and it was going to stop with me. I know now that back then there was a leader growing inside of me, and it was on a search for the truth. There had to be more than this.

I began to idolize my teachers and coaches. To me these women were confident, strong, vocal, sure of themselves—everything that I wished my mother was and that I wanted to be. Starting in middle school I would often spend hours after class volunteering in any way I could, just to spend time with them and to be a part of something. They were a source of feminine strength, and that was something I craved and searched for wherever I went.

After this drastic change in my life, I reached a level of confidence that I had never experienced, and returning to public school my senior year I felt like a new person. As I embraced the culture around me I felt less and less like an outsider. I went out for two new sports: softball and basketball. I lost forty pounds. I was finally conquering fear.

There was another change in my life as well. In my pursuit of all this strength and confidence I lacked a true idea of what self-worth really was, and I simply couldn't understand why I should hold off on sex until marriage—I had no concept of its importance. During this time I gravitated toward any guy who would pay attention to me, and I lost my virginity when I was seventeen to a twenty-six-year-old guy I met in a neighboring town. I didn't hear back from him after the third date, and just like that it was over. In my bid for independence I cast off yet another vital piece of myself as though it were nothing.

"So Liz, where do you think you'll go to school?" Ann asked. I watched her pour me a second shot through a wisp of smoke rising from the coffee table. Spring, sitting on the couch to my left, downed her third.

Ann was house-sitting for friends, up in the mountains just outside of town. Spring and I came to keep her company, bearing gifts of weed and tequila. We were nearly adults, pretty close to moving out and getting our own places, yet this sort of escape was still very highly sought after.

I thought about her question as I absently examined the drink in my hand. "I'm thinking up north, or maybe San Francisco," I said. I was seventeen and nearly finished with high school, yet somehow such plans still seemed uncomfortably far off. I was literally counting the days before I could leave; frankly, *anywhere* would do.

"Cool!" Ann returned. "I'm thinking Berkeley! Hey, maybe we can both go and room together!" Her eyes lit up at the idea.

Spring poured herself another drink. "Well I'm going to take a year to figure things out," she said. "Maybe travel and see France or something." To me that also sounded like a wonderful idea.

We spent most of the night drinking, eating great food, and dreaming of the future. The longer we talked the more I realized that I would much rather be with my strong female friends than with any guy. Here in this warm house, up in the mountains, the smell of weed and tequila in the air and the sound of our laughter echoing on the hardwood floor, my problems back in town seemed much smaller. In my mind the school was such a little thing, and the idea of pursuing guys down there suddenly seemed so unappealing. Why was I chasing them, anyway? They couldn't give me what I had in this moment. They never made me feel this way. The hours were melting away like nothing in the presence of these friends, and it was the same as with my volunteer hours at school, where I could spend any amount of time with the strong female mentors I idolized. I had never met a single man who I could say the same about. I had spent so long pursuing these guys, agonizing over what they thought of me, and now I couldn't for the life of me imagine why I'd bothered.

Drunk and with tears welling in my eyes, it hit me.

"I'm a lesbian."

Spring and Ann looked at me for a shocked moment, but even in the silence the words rang true in my own ears.

"What do you mean you're a lesbian, Liz?" Spring finally asked. She quickly put down her drink and walked over to where I sat, the shock still visible on her face, and sat next to me. Ann stumbled after her with half a biscotti in her mouth.

My brain was still reeling from this realization. It seemed that I had finally pinpointed the source of my years of heartache. All at once it felt like I had found my identity.

"It totally makes sense," I said through my tears. "I only feel at home when I'm around strong women." I took another shot. There was a lightness in my stomach now. I know it's pretty cliché, but it really did feel like a weight had been lifted from my shoulders. Liberation—or what I thought was liberation—had come.

Excited about my new self-discovery and ready with their full support, my friends wrapped their arms around me in congratulations. Spring excitedly asked, "Are you going to tell anyone? What about your parents?"

I turned to her with a determined face. "Heck yeah, I'm telling everyone!" I said. "I've lived a lie for far too long." Feeling that this particular mountaintop was a good place to begin proclaiming my newfound identity, I stood up…and fell back down onto the couch.

Ann grabbed a blanket. "Maybe we should get some sleep first," she said as she spread it over me. "After that you can tell the world."

"Okay," I said sleepily, "but after that." Then with a happy heart (and an unhappy liver), I fell asleep.

Well, once I'd slept and given it some time, I lost a bit of my nerve. I was open about my revelation to a few friends at school, but the idea of telling my parents was still a difficult one to swallow. I also realized that while some open-minded friends would see my coming out as a sign of self-realization, much of the rest of the town would probably look at me with disdain. This point struck home a few months later when my friend's parents fired me from babysitting because they didn't want me around their younger kids. Despite my desire to shun my parents in all ways, I still had that deep-seated fear of what they would think or say. I just sort of played things day by day and hoped that it would be a long time before they found out. A far cry from shouting it from the mountaintops.

I decided to confide in one of my most respected teachers, a wonderful coach named Mary. She had taken the time to instill good practices in my life, and believed that I could achieve absolutely anything I worked hard at. When I first tried out for basketball and softball I had never played either sport a day in my life, yet she put me on each team and even took the time to coach me as though I were already a valuable player. She encouraged me even though I was still very overweight. And the two whole times I actually scored baskets throughout my basketball career she cheered along with the rest of the town. When offering college advice she suggested that I consider a top university; this notion challenged and encouraged me, as I had always considered myself to be rather unintelligent and overall not good enough for anything but perhaps a lower level college or trade school.

I'd gone to Mary for advice in a lot of situations, and her perspective was usually objective and logical. And since she herself was a lesbian, I needed her advice more than ever.

I was too nervous to ask for this sort of meeting, so one of my friends approached her for me and we met in her classroom after a game one day. My heart was pounding when I walked into the room, and I could see by the look on her face that she was very uncomfortable. There, talking with the pastor's daughter about sexuality, was probably the last place she wanted to be. And this is a point I want to make really clear right now: my coach did not prey on me, seek me out to indoctrinate me with the "gay agenda," try to seduce me, or anything along those lines. I sought her out, and she saw a girl who was confused and asking for help, so she listened.

We sat and I explained where I was at. She listened closely, and wasn't quick to give advice. When I was done, she opened up about the difficulties she faced when she first came out—the turmoil it caused in her life and the lives of those around her. She told me about her thankfulness that her mother had supported her during that time. At that point she broke down crying and said, "But my parents weren't ministers." Her eyes said it all to me. They spoke of years of being rejected by society, and especially by those of the Christian faith.

Unfortunately for me, word travels fast in a small town—especially when the gossip is as juicy as a pastor's kid turning out gay.

Despite my new aversion to religion, I was still expected to go to most Sunday services. One Sunday after the sermon I was approached by one of the ladies. Her eyes wouldn't meet mine and she spoke quietly so as not to be heard by anyone else.

"Liz, I heard something from one of the girls the other day, and I wanted to ask you about it."

My heart started racing. It had only been a matter of time before it reached the church.

"What did you hear?" I asked, perhaps too quickly. I didn't want to scare her away, but I looked her directly in the face, waiting for her answer.

She looked back at me. "I heard you were…" Then her voice became a whisper: "…a lesbian." Then her eyes returned to the ground.

Alarmed, I looked around the room, as though everyone in the building was discussing the same thing we were. Mom and Dad were talking with an older couple over by the pulpit. Everything still appeared to be normal.

"Do my parents know?" I asked. My mouth was suddenly too dry.

She paused, and then said, "You know, Liz, I love you very much and it doesn't matter to me. You'll always be my sister, and—"

I cut her off, nearly yelling in my panic: "Did you tell them?"

She looked me in the eyes. "Yes," she said quietly. By the look that came over her face I could tell she was bracing for impact. "Please don't be mad at me," she pleaded. "They were going to find out soon enough; it's all over the place. I only brought it up because I thought they already knew…" She put her hand lovingly on my shoulder.

"No…" I shook my head slightly, my heart beating even faster now. "I'm not mad. I'll figure it out. At least you told me." Suddenly I was too frustrated to be in this place anymore, too anxious about the coming conversation. I walked out, got in my car, and drove off.

Later that night I came home to find my mom and brother gone; she had taken him to see a movie. Dad was sitting in the living room with the TV off. He had been waiting for me. I think a lot of people will back me up when I say that few things in life are more uncomfortable than having *a talk*. Doubly so when the parent has been waiting for you. With nowhere to run, I walked into the living room. I sat on the couch across from him.

"Can we talk, Gayle?" The middle name. Mom used it when she wanted me to know she was serious, but Dad always used it endearingly.

Just like with the lady at church earlier, he wasn't looking at me. His eyes were still. It was the first time in my life that he looked small.

"Yeah," I said.

"I think you know what we're going to talk about."

"Yeah, I think I know." I was trying to stay strong, but now *I* was the one who would rather have been anywhere else in the world.

"Someone told us that they heard…" He struggled with the words, almost as though to say them might cement them into reality. He finally finished: "…that you were gay."

"Yes, that's true," I said. My voice felt small and far away. My own eyes were down on my hands. Neither of us seemed to want to look at the other.

"Do you want help with this? Will you let us help you?"

This surprised me, and now I did look up. His eyes met mine, and I could see pain in them. I thought about what he said for a moment…and found that I had no confidence that my parents could help me. If their God had failed me, how could they do any better? I stood up. "No," I said sternly. "I don't want any help." And with that, I left the room.

~ ten ~

Peer Counseling

Being at home after that was a constant discomfort, so I was extremely relieved to be going with my high school peer counseling group on a retreat the following week. We loaded up the school van and drove for an hour before pulling off the highway and onto a dirt road that took us to an old farmhouse. Peach trees and gardens lined the driveway.

We parked and jumped out of the van, and the event coordinator greeted each of us with a hug before directing us to where we would be staying for the night. After we put away our luggage we all met in the house, where kids from several different schools were gathered for dinner. Mediterranean lemon chicken, roasted red potatoes with rosemary, and orzo pasta salad with organic greens all sat in rustic-looking bowls on the counter, buffet-style.

I approved of this setup. Right then I needed to eat good food and be nurtured more than anything. And there was a chocolate cake on the counter that I had my eye on from the exact moment I entered the room. It was like a sixth sense.

We were encouraged to eat with people from other schools, so I planted myself at a table with a girl and a guy who introduced themselves as Emma and Mark. No one else in my school was openly gay, so my heart leapt when I saw the rainbow patch on Emma's jacket. We talked about our favorite bands, our shared love of making art, and school. Eventually the subject of prom came up.

I hadn't given prom so much as a thought, and I told them as much as I started in on my second helping of chicken. Amongst everything that was going on in my life, it was just not important in the slightest. In years previous I'd gone with my friends, but no one ever asked to take me, and I didn't know why my senior prom would be any different. Emma and Mark seemed to be undecided on the topic.

Eventually the coordinator stood and ended dinner. Until she did so I had forgotten that this was a school function; there was a sense of safety and community here that I didn't usually get back at home. She told us to pair up with someone we didn't know for an exercise and I looked around for a partner. I was hoping to pair with Emma, but Mark got to me first and I agreed with a little disappointment. We were told to go and find a quiet place to talk for fifteen minutes each, just about anything at all that was on our minds or that we were currently facing. There was to be no trying to fix our partners here—just listening and being empathetic.

The sun was beginning to go down as Mark and I sat ourselves on an old fallen tree near a lush garden. Sensing my hesitation, he volunteered to go first.

"Well," he began, "I'm trying to figure out which college to apply for. My dad went to Sac State and wants me to go there. I don't know… I really want to go to art school in San Francisco…" He picked up a stick and started to absently peel off the bark.

"So what I hear you saying," I started in, "is that you're feeling pressure from your dad to go to a school you're unsure about." It was fun to stretch my reflective listening skills like a true peer counselor. And funny enough, it seemed to work well. He continued talking and I continued reflectively listening, and I could tell that some of the weight was lifting from him as he laid it out verbally. At the end of his fifteen minutes he threw a barkless stick back onto the ground.

"I love my dad," he said. "He just puts a lot of pressure on me. I know the right path will show itself." He turned to me. "So what about you, Liz?"

I was happy to finally have this chance to talk with someone about what I'd been going through and thinking recently. I needed to speak with someone who was neutral about it, discuss it in a no-pressure, low-emotion environment, like an adult.

So naturally, I burst into tears.

Fortunately poor Mark was a trooper about it, and he just let me do my thing. "I'm sorry," I said between sobs, "I'm just pretty overwhelmed right now." He assured me that there was nothing to be sorry about and stayed in the moment with me until I was ready to talk.

"I think I'm a lesbian," I finally managed. "I mean, like, I'm attracted to women even though I've slept with guys. Being with guys always leaves me with a sense of emptiness… But I've felt comfortable with women and attracted to them since I was young." Hearing the words in my own voice was foreign, yet comforting. "I feel really confused." With that, the crying was turned up to eleven—we're talking *snot* crying. After a while my fifteen minutes of straight crying were up and I wiped my tears on my shirt as Mark spoke.

"Wow, okay," he started. "So first of all, you're great for trusting me with this. Thank you, Liz. Second, you're not alone. I know I'm supposed to just be listening, and I'm not trying to fix you or anything, but Emma recently came out as bisexual. I think you would benefit from talking with her." I looked up at him and there was genuine warmth and concern on his face. I started to relax.

After the exercise we were given some free time to mingle. Feeling much better, I hung out with the other kids, enjoying the spirit of camaraderie in the group. I didn't know where Emma had gone off to, but just as I was thinking about looking for her Mark walked up to me.

"Hey, there you are," he said. "I spoke with Emma and she'd love to talk if you're up for it. She said to meet over by the barn." I thanked him and broke away from the group, making my way outside.

I was weirdly nervous. This was all still so new to me. I was thankful for the string of lights illuminating the path to the barn, as night had fallen and I've always been pretty afraid of the dark. When I reached the barn I couldn't see her at first, and jumped when she said my name from off to my left.

"Oh no!" she exclaimed, her hands up in apology. "I'm sorry I scared you!" We both laughed about it, and we found a place to sit on some crates by the barn door.

"Mark said that you were questioning a lot of things right now," she said; her voice was calm and friendly. "I'd be more than happy to help you process it."

I started with one of the more pressing issues on my mind. "Are you a religious person?" I asked.

"No, I'm not religious. I do believe in the earth and the elements. I identify myself as a Wiccan."

Her answer confused me. What the heck was a Wiccan? Someone who makes baskets?

"I come from a religious background," I said, pressing on. "My parents are Christians, and I know what they believe about homosexuality."

"I feel that what's important is what *you* believe," she said. "What do you believe?"

Her question threw me off, and I weighed my words for a moment before answering.

"I believe that I've been attracted to women all my life. That men don't interest me. And they don't seem interested in me, either. I think I've been fighting to be something I'm not." And that was the truth as I knew it.

"Then you have to follow what you believe to be true." She brushed her hair back behind her ear and smiled at me. I smiled back, feeling comforted.

We talked for another hour about all the things we were going through in life, trying to find humor in them as we did. Finally Mark ran up to us, smiling. "Just letting you guys know it's lights out in five," he said.

"Thanks, Mark," I said. "I really appreciate you." He gave me another smile and a nod and ran back to the house. We stood up, dusting off our jeans. In that moment I felt heard and connected, more so perhaps than I ever had in my entire life. Just as we started walking back I had an epiphany.

"Okay, this is really forward of me," I began awkwardly, "but would you like to go my school's prom with me?"

Even in the dim light I could see Emma's eyes light up. "Yes! I'd love to!"

And just like that, I had my first date to prom. And with a Wiccan girl—whatever that meant.

Coming home, I was on cloud nine. To maintain this high my plan was to stop in for a few hours, wash some clothes, then head out to stay at Spring's house, all while avoiding my parents as much as possible. I failed right through the door though, as my dad passed by on his way out to the church.

He stopped and smiled, but the discomfort of the encounter was visible on his face. "How was your time, sugar?" he asked. Regardless of how I treated him he always tried to stay connected with me.

Naturally, I stiffened up. "It was fine. I'm not staying long. Can I have some money for gas? Spring is studying for our math test and I said I would go."

Dad pulled out his wallet and handed me a ten-dollar bill. As I took it he said, "It was good seeing you. We missed you."

I broke eye contact and walked off. "Yeah, I'll see you tomorrow." I quickly made my way to my room, passing Mom and Jackie as I went. They were sitting at the table in the living room, Mom reading a book out loud, Jackie listening and kicking his legs under his chair. My heart sank a bit when I thought about how little time I'd spent with him recently. The guilt propelled me toward my room even faster, but when I was just about free a small voice halted me in my tracks.

"Sissy, can you take me to the park after my homework?" I turned and saw him looking up from his book, excited to see me.

"You haven't been around much. He misses his sister." Injecting a little guilt into the situation was the only way Mom could think of keeping me home. She obviously knew I was unhappy and going through a lot, but had no idea how to help.

"Maybe, Jackie," I said. "I have a lot to do before I leave for Spring's." Not wanting to give time for either of them to react, I headed into my room and started packing fresh clothes. Mom followed me.

"You're really leaving again?" she asked, this time the confusion plain in her voice. "Did your father say it was okay?"

"Yeah, Mom. It's fine. He gave me gas money." I looked up from my bag and saw her only staring at me, looking hurt and concerned. "Why is it a big deal?" I asked, my temper rising. "It's not like I don't live here." I continued to throw clothes into my bag. There was a baggie of weed near the top, and I quickly shoved it down before she could notice.

"You're just never here anymore. When you *are* here and you've been hanging out with your friends you're pretty mean to us."

Caught off-guard by the accusation, I shot back: "I have a life. I'm sorry if that's weird to you." I grabbed the rest of my things and stormed out of the house. My brother would have to wait until yet another day to go to the park with his sister.

The next morning Spring and I took the forty-five-minute drive over the mountain and spent the day at the beach. Even at that age, and even on such a spur-of-the-moment trip, my instinct was to plan the day out in order to enjoy it to its mathematical fullest. At Spring's request I managed to slip a trip to a local bookstore into the schedule, and after having tofu sandwiches and a smoke on some rocks by the pier we found ourselves in one of the many similar little shops along the coast. Tie-dye hangings adorned the walls, and the smell of incense was thick in the air.

We poked around for a while and Spring managed to find a few books. While she was paying for them I spotted a little wire display stand by the register. "Hey, check this out," I said with a smirk, and I picked up one of the items near the top. "I think I'm going to buy this."

Spring's eyes widened and she gave a nervous laugh as she paid the cashier. "You seriously think your parents will be okay with that?"

"No, and I don't care." I gave the cashier five bucks, got my change, and threw it in my bag.

Later that day I went home, and I wasn't in my room long before I heard exactly what I'd been waiting for.

"Elizabeth, can you come outside, please?" came from outside my room. My dad never raised his voice, and now was no different, but I could hear what was behind those words.

"Sure thing, Dad," I said. With my heart beating fast but my will strong, I opened the door to see Dad's furious eyes. We both knew what this was about, but I followed behind him out into the parking lot anyway without saying a word.

He stopped at my car and said, "Take it off. Now."

I had prepared to put my foot down. "It's my car, and I like it."

"Well, the title is in my name," he said with the same calm voice, "and I put gas in it. If you want to keep driving it, take it off *now*." With that he walked away.

I wanted to say more, but I knew he had won this battle. Keeping my wheels was a top priority, so I squatted down and peeled the rainbow "CELEBRATE DIVERSITY" sticker off of my bumper, muttering to myself as I did.

Before long it was time for prom, and for the first time I was actually excited about it. The night before I had the idea that getting corsages might be fun (if I was going to prom I might as well follow tradition, right?) so in the morning I rushed to the flower shop the next town over to see if there was still time to get something. I went inside and my heart skipped a beat when I saw Jan, one of the ladies from our church, wearing an apron and arranging flowers. I nearly turned around and bolted out of there, but it was too late; she'd already spotted me.

"Liz, how are you?" she asked. "Are you ready for tonight?" She put down her ribbon and gave me a big smile.

"Yeah, I was wondering if it was too late to buy two corsages?" I tried to say it as casually as possible. Jan knew what was going on in my life and was probably going to tell my parents about all this, but I told myself I didn't care.

"Sure, I can have them ready by five. You can pick them up then." She smiled again, though this time without looking at me, and continued with her work. I guess when you're gay you're just hard to look at.

Later that night I was in the bathroom doing my hair, and Mom walked in.

"So Jan called." Her words were once again stern. I could feel my face flushing as usual, but I kept my eyes on the mirror and kept working toward the big, curled, poofy hair I was going for. I mean hey, it needed to match my outfit: a white silk tank top with black pants. Oh...and silk gloves. No folks, I won't be serving you cocktails tonight; I'm on a date.

"She said your corsages were ready," Mom continued. "I asked her if she'd made a mistake, because I didn't know why you would need *two* corsages, but she insisted she had it right." She paused, fishing for information. I didn't take the bait.

"Cool, I'll pick them up on my way out," I said. Then I picked up my hairspray and started going at it.

"She got it wrong, right?" Mom asked hopefully. "You wouldn't need two cor—"

But her words were cut off by the massive cloud of hairspray I was unleashing upon the world. She went to ask again and I sprayed even more, enveloping both of us in a cloud of Aqua Net. She backed out of the room, coughing, and I shut the door with my foot.

"Sorry Mom, gotta finish," I called out to her. Then I put down the can and opened the window.

For all the buildup, prom itself was pretty uneventful. Emma and I went and there were no proud dances or grand proclamations or other flowery displays of our strong sexualities, which is what I think some people might have expected. We just hung out, drank punch, ate snacks, listened to the music and went home. The message was there however, even if it was a quiet one: *This is who I am now.* This was where I was finding my strength, and that was the end of it.

If only it were that easy.

~ eleven ~

On My Own

"Do you want to take this lamp? I found it in the shed. It just needs some dusting off." Without waiting for an answer, Dad sought a place for the lamp in the flatbed truck. Half the stuff in the truck seemed to have been added in this fashion. He wanted to make sure I had everything I might need in my new apartment.

Yes, the time had finally come. I was eighteen. I was leaving the nest, or flying the coop, or some bird thing like that. I had been accepted into a community college about two hours away, on the coast, and had even found a perfect one-bedroom apartment I could have all to myself. It was everything I could have hoped for…though despite my eagerness to get out of the house and the constantly-eroding nature of my relationship with my parents, I was surprised to find that my heart was sad to be leaving them behind. Once classes started I wouldn't be seeing very much of them, and as estranged as we were I would miss the familiarity of home. Most of all I would miss spending time with Jackie.

There was no turning back now, though. Not that I would want to. In the time since coming out I had fully embraced my homosexuality, and this was the final step in starting my new life. While trying to find feminine strength in myself I also shunned anything that itself was inherently feminine. That was, unless it also fit into the category of *new-agey*—incense, tie dye, bongs, that sort of thing. Yup. The Thomas family of rednecks had officially turned out a hippie daughter, albeit one with short hair. I'd had long hair my whole life, but the new me chucked it out along with the makeup.

I stuffed a box under a chair in the truck as Dad stowed the lamp. "Thanks," I said. "I only had one." I turned and saw Mom heading toward me with a few bags in her hands. Her face held a courteous smile, but it was obvious how she felt on the inside. Dad was trying his best to see me off with as much happiness as he could muster, but Mom wasn't taking it all as well. Our disconnect had grown too painful, and my leaving for college was a lot to handle.

She handed me the bags. "I thought you might want these. I don't think you have any washcloths. I packed you a lunch, too." Then she retreated back into the house.

I watched her go, and that familiar anger flared up inside me. Anger at her inability (or maybe refusal) to understand me. Anger that I could bulldoze her so easily. Anger that she wasn't stronger. These thoughts hovering over me like a cloud, I helped Dad finish packing.

Dad, Mom and Jackie rode in the borrowed truck while I led the way in my silver Ford Escort. The trip was relatively short, and we all knew exactly where we were going, but that didn't stop Dad from bringing along walkie talkies for inter-car communication (and not even Dad's tirades about the cost of batteries stopped nine-year-old Jackie from playing with the talkie the whole drive).

We arrived at the tiny apartment and unloaded. By the time we were nearly done I could see the conflict on Dad's face. Two emotions were battling it out in his heart: his pride in my milestone, and his fear of losing me. I could almost see this conflict on his shoulders, weighing him down.

When we were done and the two of us were alone in the house for a moment, he sat me down on the couch and looked me straight in the eyes. "Gayle," he said, "I've spent a lot of time praying and seeking God about all this. I've wanted to accept that this is just the way you are. That this is part of God's plan for you. But after all my praying and reading the Word I just can't. I will always love you. I will always be there for you as your father, and nothing could ever change that. But I can't accept that this is who you are—who you were made to be."

I was quiet for a moment. Then I hugged him. It wasn't the blessing I might have wished for, but in a way it still felt like a send-off. Here at the end of my childhood, and at the beginning of my new life, we both knew that my choices were now my own to make.

Finally the moving was done, and after Dad made extra-sure that everything was in order and that I had everything I needed, the three of them drove off. And just like that, I was on my own. Wanting to brush off the intensity of the previous conversation, I went inside and rushed to the phone. When a familiar voice picked up on the other end, I shouted, "I'M HERE! Can you believe we have our own apartments and are going to college?!"

"I know, Lizzie!" Jasmine shouted back. "It's going to be so much fun! I'm coming right over!"

To this day Jasmine is one of my closest friends. And it's funny that she should enter this story so far into it, because we've actually known each other since the fourth grade, when I started attending public school. We were in the same classes all the way up through high school, and were even friends, but for some reason it wasn't until our senior year that we became close.

And now we were both in a new city on the coast, going to the same college, living in apartments only a few minutes away from each other. It was almost too much excitement for my eighteen-year-old mind to bear. And in addition to all the fun we would have together, we could rely on each other for support if we ever became homesick. Knowing that we had each other certainly brought some comfort to my parents.

Everything was set, and I doubted I could have been much happier. The future, for the very first time in my life, was nothing but bright.

It wasn't long before I found my bearings in school and stuck to a routine that best suited me: go to school, hang with friends, deliver some pizzas at my first part-time job, and spend the remainder of my free time at home smoking weed and watching TV with my cat. The world was my oyster. No more awkward conversations, no more pressure to stay home, no more questions, no more being a kid. I could do anything and everything I wanted, and no one judged me. It was everything that I had hoped for and more. It was bachelorette bliss.

And it lasted for about a month.

One night I smoked my usual allotment and was settling in for a marathon of my favorite sci-fi show (I might have distanced myself from my parents' faith, but there were some things I just couldn't run from—

such as Dad's passion for Star Trek) when the phone rang. Normally I didn't answer while high, but for some reason on this night I did. I picked up the receiver and gave my straightest "Hello?"

"Honey, I need to talk to you. It's important." My dad's voice, so low it was hardly recognizable. Holding back tears. My breathing stopped, and the whole world seemed to go silent for a terrible moment, as if waiting for what came next.

"Your mom has breast cancer," he said. "She starts chemotherapy next week. They're hoping they caught it in time." He began to sob.

Those words rang in my ears: *Your mom has breast cancer.* Such a short thought, but the weight of it seemed to drape itself over my whole being. I don't know if you've ever had to hear such news, but when you do your mind struggles under the power of it. The moment stretches long.

"I'm coming home," was all I could think to say.

"No." Dad tried to pull himself together. "There's nothing you can do here. Grandma and Grandpa are on their way to help with Jackie, and we have plenty more help with the church members. Stay and we'll call if we need you. You're all set up there; school is your priority."

"Okay," I said distantly. "If that's what you think is best."

He told me he loved me, and I told him I loved him, and we both hung up. I sat on my bed for a long time. My brain was still struggling with the reality of it; I was shocked, but I didn't feel much yet. After a while though I sobered up, and finally I cried. The magnitude of it all hit me like a ton of bricks, and for the moment continuing to go about my job and my classes seemed like it would be impossible. For once, home was where I wanted to be.

～ twelve ～

Sinking Ship

I went home each weekend, to try and help in any way I could. When you have a loved one who's sick it seems that there's nothing in the world you want more than to help. Even if you're not helping that person directly you just hope there's any small task you can do for anyone else involved. Everything else in life feels frivolous.

Mom began her treatments, and it wasn't long before her hair was gone, as well as most of her strength. Her already small frame shrank even further. One evening was particularly difficult for her, and she was throwing up a lot. Dad was having a hard time emotionally, so I stepped in. During one of the many times I got her back into bed that long night, a deep remorse settled into my heart.

I covered her frail body with a blanket and bent over her. "Mom," I whispered. "I am so sorry. One day I hope to be as great as you are." Tears rolled down my cheeks. She looked into my eyes and squeezed my hand with what little strength she had. She was smiling.

"You were just acting your age." Her voice was weak, wavering. "It's okay, honey. I forgive you."

That night I lay awake on the couch while the rest of the house slept. Suddenly the God of my parents was the only person I could turn to, and I pleaded with Him not to take my mother. I promised that I would change, I would be a better person. I had been too awful for this to happen now. The remorse I felt ate at my heart, and it was unbearable.

The doctors soon discovered that the mass had progressed into Mom's lymph nodes and they ordered another round of chemo. They explained that she had a rare form of breast cancer that was spreading very aggressively. Since her sister had a mastectomy, Mom had been diligent about getting a mammogram every year, so they had caught it at a very early stage. But the way the cancer was reacting to the treatment, that hardly seemed to matter at all.

It was about a week before Christmas and I was at my apartment. I decided I would check in and called the house. The voice that answered was familiar, but it wasn't that of my dad or grandparents. I was surprised to find that it was my aunt, who lived six hours away. I asked why she was there, but even as I did so my heart sank.

"We just got here." Her voice was tired, and she sounded upset—my aunt, who was normally an immovable pillar of strength in my eyes.

"Dad didn't tell me you were coming. What's going on?" My breathing was fast now. I had lapsed into a panic state.

"Elizabeth, you need to come home. It's not good. They're…just making her comfortable now." She hung up the phone.

The reality of this tried to crush me, to bring me to the floor, but I was able to fight it off for the moment. I could keep moving as long as there was something to be done, and right then my whole mind was focused on getting home as quickly as possible.

The problem was that there was no gas in my car, and I would need money for food and other necessities when I got to Wilsonville. My financial aid money for the next semester hadn't been released yet and I didn't get paid from my pizza delivery job for a few days. Without knowing what else I could do, I called Jasmine.

In tears and suddenly feeling extremely powerless, I told her what was going on. She told me that I wasn't alone, and that we would be able to handle this together. Being a poor college kid herself she didn't have anything to lend me, but she took charge of the situation and brought me to the school's administration building. Running into the financial department, it was all I could do to stay calm.

The curly-haired woman at the counter called for the next person in line, and Jasmine and I hurried up. "I was wondering if I could get an early release on these funds, please?" I tried to stay calm and diplomatic as I showed her my paperwork.

She looked at me as though I'd blown all my money on booze and pop rocks. "Well, there are only a few special circumstances in which we'll release funds early," she said apprehensively. "Take this form and fill it out." She handed me some papers and called for the next person.

I stood my ground. "My mom is dying of cancer and I have to get home *now*!" I blurted out, and I broke down crying.

Jasmine put her arm around me. "Oh, honey, it's okay." She turned to the woman, whose judgmental look was now gone. "Is there any way you can make this happen, please?"

"Absolutely," the woman said. "I'm so sorry." She took minimal information and cut me a check right then and there for an advance.

As I rushed home, battling with my panic, I took comfort in the fact that I had Jasmine. To have a friend that will take care of you during the hardest point of your life… *Grateful* hardly begins to describe it.

At home I watched the ritual of death, and it was both tragic and poetic. In those two weeks all the members of the church came to say their goodbyes. Some cried because of the friendship that would be lost; I imagine some might have cried because of how they had treated her in the past; others cried because they were losing a mother. My dad caught some of it on film one day: a little town, but a grand procession of people saying goodbye. The camera gave him something to hold onto.

The food was naturally a spectacular display. If you know anything about church ladies, it's that they're always armed and ready for these kinds of circumstances. At any given time the kitchen was packed to the brim with a plethora of meats and cheeses, cookies, cakes, and that works-for-any-and-all-events churchgoer's staple, the casserole. You could bet that our fridge contained five different versions of every type of casserole you could ever imagine. The problem with grief though is that it tends to rob you of your appetite. Even amid this grand banquet I found that for the first time in my life I just wasn't interested. The only sensations my body would allow were the deep ache of the coming loss and the shortness of breath that came in moments of panic.

I didn't leave the house for days. Cabin fever had set in, making the grief even worse, but the fear of her dying while I was away was too great. I spent all the time I could manage at her bedside, and prayed that I could be with her when she passed.

One afternoon there was a knock at the door. Up to this point my friends had all given me a lot of space—partially out of respect, partially out of just not knowing what you do when your friend's mom is dying. On this day however, they mustered up the courage to come and rescue me.

My friend Emily knocked on the door and my grandpa let her in. "Come on, Liz. We're leaving." She grabbed my coat from the hook, then grabbed my arm, urging me toward the door.

"I really don't think I can leave…" I looked over to Grandma, who was in the living room. Our eyes connected, and she stood up, walked over, grabbed my other arm and helped Emily lead me to the door.

"Everyone will be here when you get back," she said. And with that, I stopped fighting. I was totally exhausted, and I could no longer fend off the urge to just get out of the house.

An old and unfamiliar Subaru Forester awaited us in the church parking lot, and it was packed with my other friends: Ann in the passenger's seat, Sara in the back, and Spring at the helm.

"Where are we going?" I asked. I squeezed in between Sara and Emily and strapped on my seatbelt, and Spring jetted us off.

"Just sit back and relax," Spring said, and the car swerved off the road a little as she searched the dash for a tape to put in.

"Oh my god!" Sara yelled. "You're going to kill us, Spring! Watch the road!" She rolled her eyes and lit the cigarette in her mouth.

"What are we doing, anyway?" Ann asked as she leaned back and lit her own cigarette off of Sara's. "Why are we being so mysterious?" I watched as she took a drag and let it out in a cloud of smoke. After being in the sterilized environment of the house for so long the smoke and the loud music were comforting—like a little taste of the youth and rebelliousness I had been missing out on.

The car came to a fork in the road. Left meant civilization via the highway; right meant private properties, empty fields, and miles of winding pothole-ridden back roads. Spring went right. I thought maybe we were going to the beach. In any case the other girls gave up on questioning our destination, so I just sat back and enjoyed the smoky air.

After about twenty minutes of driving through nowhere, Spring slowed down...then sped up again. She kept slowing and speeding erratically, giggling as she did so. And actually, this wasn't unusual behavior for her. I smiled inwardly at her silly attempt to lighten the mood, and I stared down at the car's stained carpet as I reflected on how she was such a good friend.

Suddenly Spring's voice cut through my thoughts: "Brace yourself!" Before I could even process her words or react accordingly, we crunched into an old pole and the car came to a sudden stop.

I bumped my head on the seat in front of me. Sara's cigarette dislodged on impact, and she began frantically looking for it as she yelled, "What the hell are you doing, Spring?" She found it on the floor and looked around at the rest of us. "Oh my god, are you guys okay?"

Spring began to back up, and it seemed that she was getting us out of there...until she switched out of reverse and headed once more for the pole.

"Spring, stop! You're gonna kill us!" Ann, usually quiet, was now yelling and grabbing Spring's shoulder. All our helmswoman did was laugh. For a moment even I was distracted and shocked enough to laugh with her.

We struck the pole again, and when the car stopped we all hopped out to look at the damage. A massive white dent on the bumper, shining in the sun. Everyone goggled at it, feeling dazed, while Spring pulled out her (enormous 90's) cell phone and made a call. While she dialed I looked out into the meadow behind us. We were on a stretch of logging roads that were rarely used, and it was very peaceful. It was unavoidable that I would be reminded of what waited for me back home.

Sara put her arm around me. "Are you okay, Liz? She's an idiot. I don't know why I ever get in the car with her." She glared over at Spring, who was now talking with someone.

"Yeah, I'm fine. Whose car is this, anyway?" We all walked up to Spring, who was now laughing with whoever was on the other end of the call. "You're sure, Rodger? You really don't need it? Because we're capable of a lot, here!" Her eyes met mine for a moment and she shot me a quick wink. Then she said goodbye to Rodger, hung up, and jumped up onto the car. The hood bent under her weight.

She stood tall, spread her arms wide like a superhero, and proclaimed, "I shall destroy this car!"

What came next is a bit of a surreal memory, and to this day I'm surprised that I actually got back into that thing. Rodger had told Spring that he didn't want his old beater anymore, and that she could have her way with it. Destroy it. So for about an hour Spring proceeded to drive the car into trees, over massive potholes, through old fences, and at one point into a gravel pit, all with us squeezed in with her. Each impact shook us, knocked us together, got us giggling or screaming or a nervous combination of both. My mind never fully left my mother, but that somehow made this all the more strange—like a dream. My life had come to this odd moment in time, where my mom was on her deathbed at home, and I was riding in a car that was being purposefully and systematically wrecked. The grief mixed with the reckless danger formed a concoction of emotion that could only be described as bizarre.

I tell you, they don't build them like they used to. When we were done the bumper was barely holding on, but the car was still running just fine, so the girls thought the next course of action should be to drive forty minutes up the road to see a movie.

"I really don't know if I should," I said as we pulled onto the highway. The idea of the car pooping out halfway was definitely on my mind, but more than anything I was feeling the need to get back.

"Everything will be fine, Liz," Ann said, lighting another cigarette. "Being out is good for you. I heard Titanic is good, want to see that?"

"That's about the big boat that crashed, right?" I asked. "Should be pretty action-packed. Nothing too serious, huh?"

Spring was applying a layer of lipstick in the rear view mirror as she drove. "Yeah, Liz. Just relax. I'm sure it's a fun movie."

Giving in, I settled into my seat for the ride. Maybe they were right. I should take this time to just chill out in the presence of my friends. The movie sounded like it would be entertaining enough, and I would be back in a few hours.

We arrived at the theater, and for three purely agonizing hours I watched as thousands of people drowned in icy water, fought for survival, and wept over their lost loved ones. All I could think about was getting out of there, yet it just stretched on and on. It all felt too close to home. My life was a sinking ship.

Getting out of the house had been a good idea, but by the time my friends dropped me off, the gesture had overstayed its welcome and my guilt at leaving had grown too strong. I ran into the house, but Grandma assured me that nothing had changed. Mom was still in a comatose state.

At 2:30 that morning I awoke from a dead sleep. I was suddenly struck with an urgent need to check on Mom. I jumped out of bed and made my way to her room, where I found Grandpa sitting with his laptop, likely trying to occupy his mind in order to stay awake. We all took shifts so she would never be alone.

He looked up at me. "She's been quiet for a few minutes," he said softly.

I walked up to Mom's bed and looked down at her.

"Grandpa, I think she's gone."

It was January 2nd, 1998—five days after her forty-eighth birthday and only four months after the initial diagnosis. I was nineteen and my brother was ten.

Jackie and I had bought Mom a Christmas present, though she had been too ill to even open it. It was a simple gold cross with a diamond in the center—just her style. We arrived at the funeral home and gave the cross to the director. We asked that it be buried with her, just as we knew it would when we picked it out.

We had time to view the open casket and say our goodbyes before the procession started. We watched as Dad wept over her, and tried his best to get through the beginning of what would be a difficult day. When he went off to continue business, Jackie and I went to see her ourselves, holding hands for comfort.

I don't think either of us knew what to expect. Grief wanted to grip me, pull me down…but there was something else that grabbed our attention. We stood there and stared silently for a moment. Then Jackie looked up and asked in the straight-forward way that only a ten-year-old can: "What's that on her head?"

They had fitted Mom with a wig and had failed spectacularly at matching her naturally curly hair. On another person it might have looked somewhat normal, but on Mom it just didn't work.

"It looks like a bird's nest," I said, and I had to put my hand over my mouth to hold in the giggles that were welling up. Both of us, in fact, had to try our best to keep it together. We'd expected that seeing her for the last time would be hard, but we walked away from the casket smiling. Mom would have thought it was funny too.

By the time the service started the small funeral home was packed with people. It was led by Dad's best friend, who was a pastor in a nearby town; he and his wife were friends with my parents back when they were all in college. Even now we remain close, and I'm so thankful for them.

People stood one by one and spoke about how much my mom had influenced them. I played a song on the piano that I had written, and I took pictures. Photography was, and still is, a passion of mine, and being behind the camera gave me a sense of security. It was something I knew well and could control in this very uncertain environment.

She was buried in the town's little cemetery. Some community members outside of the church raised enough funds to cover the funeral costs, and this was a gesture that impacted my dad greatly. Cards and letters poured into our mailbox in the days that followed. Torrents of cakes and casseroles found their way to our kitchen counter. Mom might have been the pastor's wife, but she touched the lives of so many both inside the church and out, atheist hippies and Christian rednecks alike.

Mom was loved.

thirteen

One with Nature

The wrought iron gate was tall and surrounded by bushes. I pulled up to it and jumped out of the car to wrestle with the padlock. As I popped it open I thanked the sun for being high in the sky; even at the age of nineteen I still dreaded opening this gate at night. My fears were never logical, either. Was I afraid of evil men waiting in the bushes to jump out and kidnap me? Or maybe of some spooked-out paranoid local who was wandering the woods? Some person on a bad trip? No. When I was alone, in the dark, facing a locked gate, I was afraid of one thing: aliens. Well, unstoppable alien monsters that were annihilating the human race, to be specific.

Jasmine's family home sat in a dense wooded area. It was right off the highway, but you didn't have to travel far down the road to forget that you were still somewhat near civilization. When I successfully opened the gate and headed on my way, I unbuckled my seatbelt, turned off the stereo, rolled down the windows, and just listened to the crunching of rocks under my tires as I always did. It reminded me of how my current life in the city was always polluted with noise. When I crossed the wooden bridge and passed the rusted-out 50's Ford truck I knew I was close. Deer grazed on the steep hills around the road. The sun warmed my short hair through the sunroof. It was therapeutic.

I pulled up to the house and squinted my eyes at the late summer sunlight reflecting from the array of solar panels off to the right of the driveway. The house before me was, and still is, one of my favorite places to visit—an old converted train caboose that's been added onto here and there over the years, nestled amongst the trees. Each room seems to hold a story: the upstairs loft where the kids had once slept and played, the living room overlooking the mountains, the bathroom where I'm always scolded for using too much toilet paper, the kitchen where the family shares good food and much laughter.

Lynn, Jasmine's mom, emerged from a gated garden further up the driveway and made her way toward me with a great big smile as I got out of the car.

"Lizzie! How was your drive, honey?" Her brown and silver curls danced as she brushed dirt from her jeans, then she gave me a hug. I could smell the distinct aroma of what I'll call Lynn's "alternative business." The hug was tight and ended with a kiss on the cheek. Sometimes that kiss would hit my mouth instead, and sometimes I even had the courage to kiss back, but my hesitation always made her laugh. Mom had always said that kissing Dad was like kissing a statue. Jasmine's family, on the other hand, was very comfortable with affection.

"The drive was great," I said, and she broke off her hug and headed toward the house.

"That's great to hear. Jasmine got here right before you did, and I'm making some lunch."

I brought my stuff inside and collapsed comfortably onto the living room floor, where I was greeted by Tuna and Bear, their excited dogs. Little prisms hanging in the windows cast rainbows on the walls, where much of my photography hung. Steve, Lynn's husband, was relaxing on the couch after several hours outdoors; he's a master builder and gardener and spends a lot of time out there. The smoke from his pipe drifted about the room, giving it all a sleepy quality. The news blared and we spoke for a few minutes about politics. Steve and Lynn had raised their kids in the woods of Northern California with a passion for protecting the environment; naturally, they were no strangers to protests, sit-ins, and petitions. Their love for the land they lived on was always inspiring.

Jasmine finally came into the room. "About time you got here," she said jokingly. I stood and we hugged, but right at the end of it I pinched her side. Immediately entering into combat stance she tried to counter my pinch with an arm lock and bring me to the floor. She had a few inches on me, but I had forty pounds on her, which always won out. I brought her to the ground instead and held her arms, pinning her.

"You punk!" she yelled, but she was completely stuck. All she had were words. We started laughing hysterically, as we always did when we wrestled.

I managed to say, "Do you want a repeat of our basketball trip?" At those words she tensed up and stopped struggling. I won't go into too much detail about that fated night on a school basketball trip a few years previous, but I will say that it involved a particularly heated wrestling match and an exchange between my rear and Jasmine's face. The planets aligned that night. And I could forever use it as a warning to those who would oppose me.

"Liz, no!" Jasmine managed amid her laughter. "I give! You win!"

After our ritual match was over we all met in the kitchen for lunch—delicious beef stroganoff, which I'll never be able to eat again without being reminded of that little kitchen.

The room was small, but functional. The tiniest fridge I'd ever seen sat next to a small counter and a gas stove. Most unusual though was the lack of a microwave. The first time I visited they could have shown me a merman living in a pool out back and I would have been less shocked than when I discovered that they didn't use microwaves. How did they heat up TV dinners? How did they cook potatoes? How did they make popcorn? These questions boggled my mind.

We sat at a small table in the corner and talked about what we were currently up to as we ate. After losing fifty pounds that year, I noticed it was much easier to sit in these chairs.

"So how are your dad and brother?" Lynn asked. "I saw them at the gas station the other day. Jack's always so funny." There was no need to ask what she meant by that. If anyone ever stopped to chat with my dad and didn't get some sort of cornball joke out of him, something was wrong.

"They're good. Just watching a lot of movies and eating a lot of Chinese food. Dad told me they know him by name at Sesame Garden." Everyone chuckled at that (though it was actually true, and the waitress there always knew what he would order as well).

Lynn then stroked my shoulder lovingly. "And how are you holding up?" she asked, her eyes filled with warmth.

Lynn met my mom when Jasmine and I were in elementary school. Mom, doing any odd job she could find, was a teacher's aide in Jasmine's class. My parents loved that Jasmine was in my life, and our families always got along well. Lynn's support was a great comfort during the grieving process. Having lost her own mother at the same age, her care for me was genuine and nurturing.

I smiled at her and nodded slightly. "I'm doing okay. Thanks, Lynn."

"Well you just let us know if there's anything you need. You know you can call any time." Then she turned to Jasmine and they chatted about Jasmine's upcoming move back into town. I listened and ate, just enjoying the peacefulness of the place. The dogs played together on the back porch. Wind chimes softly sang from the front. Watching the dust dance around in a beam of light from the window, I was struck with an idea.

"Hey!" I said loudly. "Let's go down to the river!"

"Yeah!" exclaimed Jasmine. "Do you guys want to come?"

Steve grabbed his plate and took it to the sink. "Oh, count me out. I've got way too much to do today." Then he headed out the door to continue working in the garden.

We both rounded on Lynn, but she shook her head. "Oh girls, I'm tired. I put in all those starters on the hill and pulled a ton of weeds..."

By now Jasmine and I had each grabbed one of her arms, and we knew that she couldn't escape us.

"Come on, Lynn!" I pleaded. "I won't get to visit as much once the semester starts! This could be our last chance to go this year!"

She looked at each of us, and just as we knew she would, she caved. After cleaning up we grabbed our gear and headed out.

It was ninety-six degrees in the shade on the shore of the river. The view was spectacular—a huge rock, as tall as a building, sat right in the middle of the water. A hole had been carved into the middle, and the water ran through it. The impressive formation towered over us, and the river stretched out beyond it.

Now, when I had suggested heading down to the river, I didn't exactly mean that I had a lot of swimming in mind—not for myself, at least. For me there are finer joys in such a place. Exhausted from the hike down the hill, I meticulously laid out my beach towel under a tree so as not to get any sand on it. In fact, the perimeter of my sitting area was to be quarantined; all sand, bugs, rocks, etc. were eradicated so as to create a more peaceful environment in which I could enjoy nature to its fullest…and the sandwich, chips, sweets and soda that now lined my beach towel didn't hurt either. With everything in place, I was ready for my healthy outside experience to begin. Right after the sandwich.

Jasmine and Lynn ran up behind me and pounced on my back, kicking sand all over my towel.

"Are you ready to get in?" Jasmine asked, shaking my arm with purposeful annoyance.

I was examining the damage to my comfort zone, determining how long it would take to get every bit of sand back onto the ground. "I'm good for a bit. I just want to eat and look at my magazine."

"Okay, but we're coming back for you!" The two of them ran off down the hill, and a few moments later I heard them splash into the water. I knew that Jasmine was serious, too. I might have bought myself fifteen minutes, tops, but they would be back, and they probably wouldn't relent until I got into that water.

Compared to the foggy coastal city I lived in, the dry heat was relaxing, and it was hard to read my magazine without drifting off. Plus the Jelly Bellies and chips took their toll on my energy. I'd lost a lot of weight, but still had the occasional candy binge when I wanted to have a good time.

My self-induced coma slowly lifted as the sound of laughter came up the hill.

"Come on, Lizzie!" Lynn called.

"Just five more minutes," I tried to call back, though it came out as more of a loud mumble. I helped myself to another handful of Jelly Bellies before plunking my head back down onto my towel.

Lynn and Jasmine were standing next to me now, and something about the way they were giggling was unsettling. I raised my head and beheld them in all their glory: two grown women, butt-naked, looking down at me with expectant faces.

"Skinny dip with us, Lizzie!" Jasmine said. "You'll love it!"

I wanted to just get up and run. It didn't matter where—I just needed to get out of there. I was completely mortified by the very idea. And before you throw down the book and run to wash your eyes, this had nothing to do with sex; it was about being comfortable in my own skin.

Naturally I'd always been insecure when it came to my own body. In high school volleyball I always waited until all the other girls were on the bus before I showered. One time I gathered up the courage to just go in and shower while another girl was in there. I proclaimed to the world: "This is my fat, and I'm not hiding it anymore!" and marched right in there wearing nothing but my flip flops. My pride quickly melted into shame when I looked over at the other girl and saw that she was just standing there, gawking at me, mouth hanging open. The petite girl, with about two-percent body fat, was transfixed on my big stomach. Wanting to break the tension I looked right at her and said, "This is what you have to look forward to after you have kids." She didn't get the joke.

Jasmine and Lynn reached down and grabbed my arms (a distant part of my brain was aware of the additional sand they kicked on my stuff) and hoisted me up, pulling me toward the water.

"Come on, live a little!" Jasmine said. "It's so freakin' good out there!"

Finally my wits were coming back to me. "No way, I am *not* doing this!" I tried to pull back, but they kept on strong. Peer pressure is a heck of a thing. When we were at the edge of the river they finally let go, and they stood ankle-deep in the water.

"Come on, sweetheart," Lynn said, more softly now. "You're beautiful and you have nothing to be ashamed of. And we won't look while you get in, we promise." She got into the water and turned around, motioning for Jasmine to do the same. The sun warmed their backs as they awaited my decision. Now was my chance to escape, and put this idea behind me for good. I could return to my magazine and my sandwich and my jelly beans and my safe little bubble in the shade…

Yet crazily, I found myself considering it. Their enthusiasm was just so contagious—their freedom to be uninhibited and carefree, to not worry about being seen or about little bugs getting in their crevasses. All of a sudden that sort of freedom sounded wonderful.

"Okay," I found myself saying, "I'm going to get in the water, *then* take my clothes off. But you still have to stay turned around!" I started into the water and was greeted with cheers.

"Alright, Lizzie!" Jasmine shouted. They egged me on as I got in and disrobed.

And I'll tell you right now, that water liberated the chubby, frightened volleyball girl that still lived inside me. My clothes were tossed up onto the shore, yet there was no staring, no teasing, and no snickering behind my back. Just three friends splashing in the water and enjoying the thrill of the adventure. Throwing fears of bugs and of my foot touching algae to the wind, I was one with nature in true hippie fashion.

~ fourteen ~

Weed and God

Returning to school, I sought to make sense of my life. Still grieving and attempting to find community in this new town, I attended the LGBT group at the nearby university and spoke with one of my professors—a lesbian—about what was going on in my life. The group was a place where I could talk without people judging me, and I was very thankful for that. There was, however, an undertone of loneliness at the meetings. I think much of it was due to the fact that each semester new students joined and left the group, making it harder to stay connected. It was an ever-contrasting feeling of both hope and isolation.

One day my professor asked if I was interested in joining a panel of LGBT students who spoke to classes. And of course, I jumped at the chance! "*Sure, I've been out of the closet for…*" *looks at watch* "*…about a year now, and I think that does validate me as an expert in the field.*"

One panel discussion was for a sociology class. Five of us sat in front of the class as the students asked questions. I had been excited about the opportunity, but that excitement soon fizzled when the realization that I was in front of so many peers sunk in. My cheeks reddened as I waited for my turn to give a short summary of who I was. They always feel hot and red when I'm nervous.

My turn came, and one student asked me, "So if your dad's a pastor, how does he feel about all this?"

Suddenly I was torn between embracing my sexuality and defending my father. To me it was a complex question. I answered, "He doesn't believe it's who I am, but he loves me." Some of the students shook their heads in disapproval.

Eventually I found another apartment a little closer to school and shared it with a couple of friends of mine named May and Alex. At first I had reveled in having my own space, but after Mom died it was nice to have them in my life—to be able to come home to people who cared about me and helped keep my emotions intact. May even taught me invaluable lessons in cleanliness, which was something I'd been neglecting amid my grief. Dad was known for his impeccable cleanliness, and with my rebellion toward all things holy I'd left the mop behind. But May made me pick the mop back up and taught me about taking ownership of my environment. She also taught me a lot about health and nutrition, and after enduring such constant negativity regarding my body from other kids growing up, it was so refreshing to have a kind friend who didn't criticize, but only demonstrated healthy habits. Her boyfriend Alex taught me guitar, and we would sit and smoke and play music together.

One day, with my new roommates gone and my morning free, my goal was similar to that of most days like this one: fill the living room with smoke, watch a movie, and check out. I sat on the couch, staring at the TV, my cat weaving through my legs in a bid for attention. Remembering the last time Mom ever saw him, I quickly took another hit off my three-foot bong and forgot about my pain.

It had been fifteen months since she died. Grief and remorse kept me busy most days. My routine was becoming progressively more difficult: During the day I did as little work as possible to pass my classes, and at night I got high and delivered pizzas. Luckily most of the staff was high too, so no one ever responded to the complaints.

I was incredibly thankful that I had enough weed for the rest of the day. I had four more hours before my roommates would be home, and I intended to use those four hours. I tried to zone out on the TV…

Yet despite the weed I was becoming painfully aware of my heart's condition. It had always been the elephant in the room that I tried to ignore, but it wasn't just in the room anymore; now the elephant was on my chest, beating me with its trunk and its tusks. The more I tried to zone out the more acutely aware I became of just how broken I felt. Weirdest of all, I found myself thinking about God.

My approach to God had always been one that was based on performance. Countless times as a child I was the first to arrive at a church service and the last to leave, all in an effort to find Him. I would put myself as close to the action as possible. But when it came to the condition of my heart, God was far from me. I had watched my parents struggle and experience much loss. Poverty surrounded us, and even though we were sometimes gifted with miraculous provisions, I longed for more. I sang the songs about being unconditionally loved, about selling out for Jesus, about giving it all away because of His love for me... Yet the posture I approached Him with was one that was always ready for punishment. I chased after God with my actions, yet I never truly opened my heart to Him. I didn't think that was what He wanted. Now, after leaving the Church, I continued to look for shelter from pain in any way I could, whether it was the numbing intoxication of drugs, sex, or a culture that was a complete contrast to the one I was raised in. Now more than ever, I left Jesus locked outside as I ran.

I had recently started seeing someone, and she once asked me why I didn't have my faith displayed. She was Catholic, and a picture of Jesus was taped to the wall by her bed. I told her I preferred to keep Jesus off-display; I was more comfortable with Him in a box in the closet, buried under a stack of my dusty old Carmen CD's.

I mulled over all of this as I sat there, feeling perhaps the most miserable I'd been in my entire life. I felt like I had nothing, and though I had continued to run, I had nowhere to go. For the first time I opened myself up to God—not as though He were an angry father, but as though He were my own father, sitting next to me. For once I decided to be real with Him.

"Um, I know I'm high," I said to the empty, smoked-filled apartment. "I'm probably not supposed to talk to you when I'm high, but I really have nothing to lose. I'm in this pretty deep. I've burned a lot of bridges, I've lost my mom... I have nothing."

What happened next floored me. It bent my perception of God and of who He was—permanently.

A warm presence filled the room. It poured into my chest like water. I heard no audible words and saw no angelic presence, but I could literally feel His response to my prayer. That response was warmth; it was a feeling of the love that He felt for me, and had always felt, and it seemed as though my depleted soul was taking a huge drink. My old theology was out the window. Everything I knew of Him began to change in that moment, and when this heavy presence subsided it left me with the hard knowledge that my world was shifting. It was the starting point. This was the desperate plea, the act of humility that He needed in order to begin.

I wish I could tell you that this is the part of the story where the glorious revelation cures me of all my problems, and I live happily ever after. That's how these things normally work, right? Aren't we often taught that all you have to do is find God and your life will be perfect? I wish I could thank you for reading, tell you to drop me a line sometime and say so long for now. But I can't. As I said, this was a starting point—and that's a far cry from a happily-ever-after.

Over the course of the next few days I kept my normal routine. Go to school, come home, smoke. I'd had a legitimate encounter with God, yet wasn't really expecting any immediate changes. Stupid, stupid, stupid.

My routine was being forcibly interrupted, however, whether I wanted it to be or not. Massive panic attacks and feelings that I was literally dying when I smoked sort of messed things up for me. One of the last times I ever smoked was right before a drive to see my dad and brother. I wished that I could burst into the house and proclaim my newfound faith and start living as part of a happy family again, but there was still so much painful awkwardness between us, so I medicated. By the time I arrived I was sober enough to have a conversation but numb enough to disconnect, as was usually the goal. This time was particularly bad however, and the topic of God never came up. After only a few minutes of sitting at the dinner table I felt as though I physically couldn't be there anymore and made an excuse to leave. My heart was pounding as Dad and Jackie followed me out to the car. Dad didn't say anything or try to stop me from leaving; he only waved sadly as I drove off. Much later he would tell me what Jackie said that night—that he would always love me, but those days it was hard to *like* me. It was a difficult moment for everyone involved.

A few nights later, however, a phone call brought a lot of relief to my dad's broken heart. Sober and in a ton of pain I called him, and he was obviously surprised to hear from me.

"Hey there, Gayle!" he said. "How are you doing?"

"I'm good," I lied, trying to keep my voice steady. "Hey, Dad... So you know how I'm saving up money for that trip to Maui with my friends?"

"Yeah, this summer, right?" He probably thought I was just asking to borrow some cash.

"Yeah. So, instead of going to Maui, I've decided I'm going to Pensacola."

There was a long pause. He was at a loss for words.

Before Mom died they had taken a trip to Pensacola, Florida, to experience the massive movement of God that was taking place there. To us small town folk with our tiny church, Brownsville Assembly of God was the Big Time—the place to which anyone who truly wanted to experience God made a pilgrimage. I knew it was where I needed to go to find Him.

Dad of course immediately knew what my going there meant. "Um, okay," was all he could manage to say at first. Then, after another moment: "We're going to trust in God that you'll get the funds to go. I love you. I'm so proud of you." His voice was filled with relief. I told him I loved him and hung up the phone.

Jackie later told me that he walked into the living room to find Dad holding the phone, weeping. This scared him, as the last time it had happened had been when the doctors called about Mom's cancer. But Dad told him I was coming back to the Lord.

Two months later I was on a plane, and fear ripped through my body. Convinced that Jesus now had me where He wanted me and that the plane would plummet to the ground halfway through takeoff, I thanked Him for my salvation. I heard a voice say, "You're going to be okay. You're safe." The fear didn't leave, but this was the very beginning of hearing Him in a new way—it was quiet, like a small voice speaking directly to my heart.

The next five days were intense. Thousands upon thousands of people attended Brownsville during the revival that ran through the late nineties, and the crowds were unlike anything I'd ever experienced. I spent the nights alone in my motel and the days attending services, sometimes waiting in line for hours. I met people from all over the world, and it expanded my perception of the hugeness of this movement. The people were hungry, and the message in every service was the same: *Run to God.*

The experience was incredible, but perhaps the most important thing to come of it was the plane ride home. God spoke to my heart again and told me I needed to go to ministry school. Brownsville had a ministry school, so I considered that. The thought of leaving my Dad and brother to move across the country saddened me, but I was willing to do anything. Little did I know, only a year later I would be attending a ministry school with the same heart as Brownsville, and only a few hours away from my family.

～ fifteen ～

The Narrow Path

During the months following my experience in the living room, every day was a battle. In a constant fight over my devotion and my emotions, often it was all I could do to make it through the day. The results of not properly dealing with the pain of my mother's death and of my years of rejection now stared me in the face.

Medicating was no longer an option. My defense had always been to isolate myself and to plot and plan out how I would dull it all with weed, alcohol, porn, sex, and the overall fantasy of relationships. But now that had all left the arena, and the raging bull that was my pain wanted a piece of me.

I struggled with powerlessness. Because I had never felt powerful I always gave my power away, to anyone or anything that would take it. Transitioning out of that was a slow process. The girl I had been seeing called and left messages, but I was too afraid to speak to her and just didn't answer. My college mentor who headed the LGBT group wrote me to see if I was okay, but I didn't answer her either. In hindsight I probably owed them at least an explanation, but I acted like a coward.

During this time I totally abandoned the idea of ever getting married. I still felt attracted to women, and amid all the confusion I decided to adopt a nun-type mentality—just without the outfit. As usual, my response to fear was to run from it. In my eyes sexuality was harmful, and I didn't think I could be trusted with it. I did my best to focus my mind on other things. To be honest I was a little surprised that the attraction hadn't just disappeared by then, and since I still didn't have anyone asking me the hard questions, I tried my best to sweep it all under the rug for the time being.

Panic attacks consumed my days as I tried to work and continue with school. My free time was now spent in my room, reading the Bible or listening to worship music. In a fit of fearful righteousness I threw away all of my non-Christian music and movies (and later regretted it; it took me a long time to re-build my Bonnie Raitt collection). I had only found God when I stopped posturing and made myself vulnerable, yet still I was afraid of disappointing Him. I was tormented with thoughts of death, and of the feeling that something was trying to suffocate me at night—like something sitting on my chest, pressing the breath out of me, leaving me unable to cry for help. I knew in this time that there was a war being waged. Each day I quietly asked for direction.

I also reconnected with Katherine—Mom's close friend, who I used to sit with during bake sales—and she took me in with open arms. We had been so close since I was so young that being in each other's lives again after years of distance was a wonderful relief. Especially now that Mom was gone, I valued our relationship more than ever, and she took every opportunity to speak positively into my life and comfort me in this time of grief. She would later tell me that in these early days of my new journey she'd noticed a certain "softening" of my appearance and demeanor, as though I had become comfortable allowing some of my femininity to show through, perhaps without always noticing it.

Katherine's support was invaluable, but with the floodgates open and my junk now pouring everywhere, I knew that connecting to a church community would be the next step toward recovering any sense of harmony in my life. I spent a while searching for the right connections, and one day at school someone saw my Bible and told me about a gathering of different churches that met once a month south of town.

A month later I found myself pulling up to a large community building, and it was both intimidating and exhilarating. People from different denominations pulled up in their church vans and beat-up cars. Congregations from all around came together and greeted each other like groups of old friends. When worship started I settled into my place in the packed room, and later a young couple took the stage and preached for about an hour. Perhaps in an effort to preach on something that people from all different denominations could agree upon, they basically just talked about how God loves you. In my hungry state I thought it was minimizing God and His true nature, so I sat there picking it apart. A tiny wall had just gone up without me even realizing it.

At the end of the service they invited people to come up and receive prayer and experience the love of God. I moved to the front and a man with grey hair walked up to me.

"Hi," he said, smiling, "how can I pray for you?" His eyes were kind, and he smelled good.

For a moment I considered asking for a million more wishes, but I wasn't sure he would get the joke.

"I'd like to experience God's love, I guess." After I said it, I was suddenly aware of a surge of anticipation inside myself. The air felt electric.

All around me people were praying for others in pairs—one person in the front, doing the talking, and one "catcher" in the back, ready to act if the person fell. That's what the good ol' Pentecostals call being "slain in the Spirit." My father once sat me down as a child to explain what seemed to be a very strange phenomenon to me:

"When the Holy Spirit comes in contact with us, we react in different ways. Some people shake, some fall on the ground, some cry… It just depends on what God is doing. Sometimes it can seem weird, but even when it does it's not for us to judge."

As people fell all around me I thought, *Well, this guy's nice. I'll give him what he wants.* I decided I would give him what we in the biz call a "courtesy fall"—a fall that's easy and controlled. Imagine the lead dancer in Swan Lake fluttering gracefully to the ground. Once as a kid I had given falling a go and the catcher had missed, so I wasn't eager to do an encore of my Charlie Chaplin impersonation. And after being pushed over by excited preachers countless other times, my "trust fall" days were at an end.

"Okay, God," the man said, "give her what her heart desires." His hands gently touched my shoulders.

I think it was about an hour that I was lying on the floor, laughing hysterically. No memory of how I got there, how I fell, or who did or did not catch me. A presence of joy and healing began to melt my heart. As I lay there, that soft voice began to speak over me, repeating, "I love you. Don't be afraid."

Eventually I pulled myself from the floor, and a new and intense sensation came over me. I had heard people refer to this state as being "drunk" before, but had never known exactly what they meant until then. It's a weightiness and awareness of God's presence so thick that it's like being covered in a warm, wet blanket. I eventually managed to get home and I sat in my car for a long time, waiting for this feeling to pass. I still lived with my roommates, and I didn't want to act weird in front of them; they would have no grid for what was going on with me. No matter how long I waited it just wouldn't normalize though, so I decided to get inside and just go quickly to my room. With any luck they would be asleep.

Immediately upon opening the door I was greeted by May, who stood in the kitchen making a sandwich.

"Hey Liz, how was your day? You're home late."

Not wanting to rush off rudely, I walked up to the kitchen doorway and smiled at her. "Um, it was good." I tried to stay as normal as I could. You know, not like a crazy charismatic Christian.

"Cool," she said as she looked up from her sandwich. "Well I was going to take a walk tomorrow, and…" She stopped mid-sentence and stared at me for a moment. "I'm sorry," she said, "I can't be around you right now." She took her snack and went quickly to her room.

I was surprised by her reaction and tried to think on it as I retired to my own room, but exhausted and filled with the Holy Spirit I plunked down on top of my blankets with all my clothes on and fell asleep immediately. I slept more deeply than I had in years.

I woke up the next morning with my cat draped across my back and a puddle of drool on my pillow. Yes, such grace in such a glorious state. I felt incredibly well-rested, and my heart itself felt light. Sunlight filled the apartment and the whole world seemed new again as I made breakfast. May came in as I was eating and sat next to me at the kitchen table.

"Hey Liz, I'm sorry I ran away from you last night. It was like you were you, but there was some energy around you that was different. I…felt like I couldn't breathe. I had to leave." She looked down into her tea for a moment, then up at me.

I looked her in the eyes. "That was God, May. I don't know why or how, but I felt so much of God last night that it was like I was drunk. I can't believe you felt it too!" I wanted to talk about it further, but I didn't want to freak her out. I tried to hold back my enthusiasm and casually got up to wash my dishes.

Despite the implications of that experience, we never talked about it again. I knew what I had been through, and knowing that someone else had felt it too was enough proof for me that God was doing something in my life. Soon after that I found my own place closer to the church I began attending. I was back on my own, but this time with so much more to live for.

It's funny how such tiny coincidences can lead to such enormous changes. God of course knows this well and tends to use it to His advantage. I was at a friend's wedding in Sequoia, which was about four hours away, when I happened to strike up a conversation with the lady sitting next to me. We had never met before, but after learning that she was a Christian I decided to share a little about myself. (It's funny how being a Christian can be a little like being a parent, or a skydiver, or a Star Trek fan. It can feel like being in a club, because even if you're strangers you always have a lot to talk about.)

We were chowing down on hors d'oeuvres and wedding cake when she said, "I'm not sure why I'm telling you this, but there's a ministry school here in town that you may want to check out." She gave me a little more info and I said I would look into it. Neither of us could have known that we would soon be in the same class at that very school.

The months went by and I spent most of my time devouring books, reading my Bible, listening to sermons on tape and taking in anything else that spoke about God's love. I also continued to eat healthy foods and work out as May had taught me. Since my senior year of high school—when I had first begun to lose weight—I was down eighty pounds. I was almost at what was considered a "normal" weight for my height.

The pastor of my small congregation gave me a key to the church and said I could come and pray any time. The sanctuary had a large piano and I would sit and play for hours, pouring out songs to God. Songs of thankfulness, praise, and pain. It was during these times that the tangible presence I'd first felt that afternoon in my living room would come and speak to me. Sometimes it was an impression, a picture, an overall feeling of peace, and it was always a message of His love for me.

While playing one afternoon (I always came when I knew no one else was there, for I'm sure I sounded like a drunken sailor) I sang out to God, and with my song came a revelation. It's difficult to describe what went on in my brain, but it was almost like a sudden download of information. A lot of ideas flooded into my head; a lot of things clicked into place.

Without stopping to plan, I sang out what I was now realizing: "*And You wept over me while I was lost and in pain. You cried as Your heart broke because I was far from You.*" Sobbing, I played and sang with a new level of understanding of the agony He felt when I didn't know His love for me. How He couldn't comfort me even though I was hurting. How I had separated myself from Him through not believing that He was a good father.

One of my classmates found me a job as a barista at the edge of town. Finally out of delivering pizzas and into a bright new environment, the air in my lungs was starting to clear (both figuratively and literally). Two entrepreneurs with very large hearts hired me onto their small crew. With these people I felt like I could be my messy self, open with aspects of my life, even though they didn't share my Christian beliefs. Learning how to work with an excellent spirit was what I would most take away from that job.

The shop sat directly beside the busy highway, and on many days I was left running the place alone. All sorts of characters came by to get coffee and talk life. Full of new zeal and a willingness to take risks, I saw my time there as an opportunity to grow.

One day a truck pulled up to the café. Sally, a regular, got out and made her way inside. Our bosses encouraged us to anticipate the orders of our regulars, even if it meant remaking a drink every once in a while (which was always great because we got to drink the botched ones), so I started on her usual decaf raspberry mocha. Stirring in the fresh raspberry purée sauce made from scratch and the decadent white chocolate that came from actual gourmet ground white chocolate bars, I heard the Lord speak to me.

"She has migraines. I want you to pray for her." A calm presence came over my mind, but my heart began beating quickly.

"What do You mean, pray for her? I'm making her a drink. I'm not at church." Well out of my comfort zone yet wanting to be obedient, I conceded.

Back then the concept of praying for people who were sick and actually expecting God to touch them was still very new to me. My pursuit of teachings on the love of God led me to the truth that He wants to heal in many ways, and one way is healing of the body. Growing up, I did witness a lot of people in our church praying for the sick and injured. Honestly though, it was not often that we saw any healing, and I'm not sure how many people actually expected it. My parents demonstrated the love of God in a different way: through feeding the poor, counseling the lost, and caring for the flock. That was truly wonderful, but in my hunger for more, I discovered that there was much more to the complete Christian walk.

Sally had mentioned once that she was indeed a Christian, but knowing that didn't do much to alleviate the awkwardness of the moment. How do you even begin a conversation like this? Knowing that if I waited too long I would chicken out, I jumped in head-first. I heard the door open behind me as I finished her drink.

"Hi Sally, would you like whipped cream today and do you get migraines?" I tried to sound casual but the words all kind of came out in a jumble. I turned to give her the drink.

"Yes, I do want whipped cream, and...I do get migraines." As she replied the realization of what I'd said hit her. She looked curiously at me for a moment before asking, "How do you know I get migraines?"

How did I know? Good question.

I still tried to play it cool as I topped off her mocha. "I guess, well... I think God just told me because He wants me to pray for you." I handed her the mocha, and in that moment I was exceptionally thankful that no one else was in the café to hear what I was saying. I prepared for rejection as I asked, "Is it okay if I pray for you?"

Sally's eyes welled up.

"Yes, please do," was all she said, and she leaned up to the counter. I put my hand on her shoulder and said a simple prayer.

"God, thank You for this woman who loves You. Please bring Your healing power and take away these migraines." Nothing fancy. Sally began to cry, and she thanked me.

A couple weeks later, Sally came in again during one of my shifts. I greeted her with her raspberry white mocha, and she gave me a huge smile.

"Liz, thank you so much for praying for me! I normally get migraines almost daily, but these last few weeks I've only had two! It's so much better!"

To put it lightly, my mind was kind of blown.

"Sally, that's amazing! Just so you know, I've never even done that before...like, pray for someone like that! I'm so thankful that God touched you!"

She paid for her mocha and was on her way, and it felt like something had opened up inside of me. Trusting that what I was hearing was from God and stepping outside of my comfort zone gave me the confidence I needed to take further risks. It was a little like riding a bike; I did it once, so each time after was easier.

I rode that bike whenever I could during my time at the café, careful of course not to start scaring people away. The great thing is that God always knew exactly who needed prayer the most. One time I prayed for an older couple who were vacationing from Texas, and they would go on to help me pay for school and bless me in other ways as well. All from just one little conversation and a prayer.

During this time one event stands out the most, however. I met a girl named Stephanie in an English class as I was finishing up school at the junior college, and it wasn't long before we were meeting for coffee and chatting about our lives and our shared faith in God. One day she was very down and confided in me.

"It's been so awful, Liz. My husband's been in and out of jail, and he's trying so hard to stay sober. I'm trying to quit smoking weed, too. I know God wants us sober for our kids right now, especially with Michael's new medical needs…" She stared blankly at her coffee, and my heart broke for her.

Michael, her seven-year-old son, had recently been diagnosed with a disorder that made his hipbones unusually frail. He had fallen and shattered his hip, and the healing process was very slow.

I felt God nudge my heart. "Would it be okay if I came and prayed for him? I mean, I don't want to impose or anything…"

"Yes!" she instantly responded. "Can you come over this weekend?" She wrote down her address, visibly excited.

A few days later I prayed that I was doing the right thing as I rang the doorbell of the apartment. Two young girls—probably still in elementary school—opened the door, jumping around like monkeys as they did so. Stephanie came up behind them.

"These are my girls," she said with a tired smile. "There's no school today, so we are full of energy!" She led them away and brought me into the living room, where I sat down. "I'll go get Michael," she said. She walked off down the hall and came back with little Michael in her arms. She told me that he couldn't walk more than one or two steps on his crutches; the pain was too great.

She sat him down on the couch next to me, and he just smiled up at us. "Michael," she said to him, "this is Miss Liz. She's going to pray for you. I'll be right over there in the kitchen with the girls, making lunch, okay?" He nodded meekly, and she walked off.

I didn't want him to feel intimidated, so I sat down on the floor in front of him to get a little lower. I placed my hand gently on his side, and he still didn't say anything—just sat and smiled, wiggling for a moment to get more comfortable. I closed my eyes.

"Jesus, I pray that You come and touch Michael's hips. I pray that You bless him and that he would know Your love for him." Another simple one; I felt those were always the best. As I finished I opened my eyes to find Michael's face right next to mine. His arms quickly wrapped around my neck and he planted a big, wet, sloppy puppy dog kiss right on my cheek. I can still remember the force of his hug. It was one of the most adorable things I've ever experienced.

"Thank you for that lovely kiss," I laughed as I wiped little boy slobber from my face.

Stephanie and I chatted for a while, then hugged as I was on my way out. "Thank you so much for coming, Liz. It was so sweet of you to bless my family like this. To come all this way to pray for him." There was genuine gratitude in her eyes, and I left feeling lighthearted and warm.

School had ended that week, so I didn't see Stephanie for a while. After a few weeks I found that she was on my mind, so I decided to call her. She lit up once she heard who it was.

"Liz! Oh my gosh! I couldn't find your number and I didn't know where you lived, so I couldn't contact you! So you left that day after praying for Michael, right? After you left I carried him upstairs to be with his sisters in their room. A few minutes go by and they start screaming! I run up there and I see Michael walking around the room without his crutches!" Her voice cracked with excitement.

I started to cry. I was in utter shock. Despite being bold enough to pray for people there was always that niggling little doubt that my prayers were actually accomplishing anything. It was obvious that God wanted to show me that He was bigger than the boxes I put Him in.

sixteen

Stretched to the Limit

With a softened heart, I could finally begin the healing process with my family. Both my returning to the Lord and our grief over Mom brought us closer together. I was able to tear down the walls I had been building for years.

As many weekends as I could manage I would drive to Wilsonville to visit my dad and brother, and we were able to laugh and have fun as I'm sure Dad had always dreamed of. Jackie and I spent a lot more time together, which helped alleviate much of the guilt I'd felt in the latter years of high school. That summer he even came to stay in my apartment for a week. We watched movies, ate snacks, went for walks, and he washed dishes at the coffee shop for some of my tip money. (In true teenage-boy fashion, he neglected to bring more than one change of clothes, and couldn't understand why I wasn't exactly okay with that.) In a small way it was like we were really getting to know each other again.

Dad and I grew close as well. We'd always been very similar in personality and in how we responded to situations; so naturally, once my walls fell, he gladly stepped back into my life. In fact during his continued grieving period he depended on and confided in me—probably because he was uncomfortable being open with anyone but family.

He still ran the church of about thirty as best he could, but Mom had always been the church's legs. She had thrived within the congregation, had organized events, had given the place that much-needed pastor's wife level of energy. Dad's strengths were counseling, teaching, and pastoring. They had complimented each other perfectly, and without her, Dad had a much harder time keeping things running smoothly.

Naturally he was feeling emotionally lost as well. With no close friends in town and only Jackie living at home, he was lonely. Because of his weight he didn't think he would ever re-marry, and thus never had the confidence to pursue anyone. It was very sad to watch such a great man lose all hope. I did my best to encourage him, and my growing passion for God brought a lot of peace to Dad's life, but the sense of grief and isolation that I felt when visiting seemed only to increase. On numerous occasions I offered to move back, but every time he insisted that I stay in school—especially now that I was preparing to go to ministry school.

Only four hours away in Sequoia was a very large and ever-growing church with a relatively new program, which I'll call Ministry Academy, or MA. I'd enrolled and would be moving to attend in the fall…provided I could secure the funds. I had no idea how I would get the kind of money I needed, but I knew that this was God's plan for me and that He would make it happen.

One day I was walking down the path between the church and the house. Dad and Jackie were sitting on the porch reading, as they often were. I was about to head inside when I noticed an envelope taped to the screen door. I looked over at Dad, and his eyes twinkled at me. "I think there's something on the door for you," he said with a smile. Confused, I grabbed the envelope and opened it to find a wad of cash—about a thousand dollars. There was a note that read, "*Here is the beginning of the money you need for school.*" By now I was flipping out, staring at the money in amazement. That was nothing however compared to when I read the second line on the note:

"*For your next clue, go to the office.*"

"Dad!" I shouted. "What is this?! How did you get this?!"

"Just keep going," he said. I hurried into the house and he followed behind me.

In Dad's office (formerly Jackie's room, formerly the dining room) I found another envelope with another wad of cash...and another cute note. With each envelope my hype level rocketed further and further into the stratosphere, and by the time I opened the fourth and final note, my first year of school was completely paid for and I was in tears. This last one had been taped to the bathroom door and I sat in the hallway, looking down at the money and thanking God for His goodness. Dad came up behind me.

"One of our members donated that to cover your tuition and get you started." He beamed down at me, having taken considerable joy in planting each bit of money. Those sorts of little games and surprises were his style, and even now I can't give someone a large present without making a big play out of it.

I counted the money again, as though I was going to look down and find that they were all really one-dollar bills. But it was all there, everything I needed to get to Sequoia. With my finances set, school would officially be starting in the fall. Unfortunately, that meant that my commute back to Wilsonville would double, so I wouldn't be able to come home and support my family as much. I had to trust that God would take care of them as I continued on the path He was laying out for me. My brother, now twelve, was particularly hard to separate from for long periods.

The time finally came and Dad loaded up the borrowed truck once more to move me, and despite Mom's absence there was a new spirit of hope and connection between us. I felt a pang of guilt when I realized how much tension I had once caused in my family, but quickly reminded myself that those thoughts were purely unhealthy; sometimes it can feel like my own mind would wreck itself with guilt and regret if I let it, and I'm sure a lot of others feel the same way.

A very kind woman whose son attended my previous church managed an apartment complex in Sequoia and let me stay with her until my own apartment opened up a few months later. And just like that, I was once more in a new town, going to a new school, on my own. It was even more exciting than the first time, and also a lot scarier.

Once school started it was immediately apparent that I was going to be stretched at all angles.

MA isn't like a traditional university; it's focused on ministry, as opposed to the sort of Christian college that my dad went to. Instead of being separated into smaller classes and taught on very specific subjects, we spent the whole day together as one big group of about seventy people. Our teachers and a number of other speakers would come in and teach on a variety of topics. Our pastor's core belief was that everyone deserved an encounter with God, and that we had a mandate to bring that encounter to them through a lot of different expressions. As such, part of the curriculum involved going out into the community and offering any help we could give. In the poorer neighborhoods we offered to pick up garbage, mow people's lawns, cook hot dogs for kids—anything we could practically do that might demonstrate God's love. The church understood that simple acts of kindness are some of the most powerful weapons in our arsenal. Many of the people we helped were completely baffled and visibly touched that we would give of ourselves in exchange for nothing.

Since MA was part of a church, we were required to attend at least two services a week. For me this level of discipline in seeking God was extremely beneficial in walking out my new freedom; the routine and the homework and the forced group interaction helped keep me walking the path I knew I had to walk. It made it nearly impossible for me to isolate myself. And despite how busy I was, my work never got in the way of seeking out God. To me it seemed the perfect balance.

One very important thing that I quickly learned from school was the fact that God is always speaking, and it's up to us to hear and respond. I learned that He speaks in many different ways, and in class it was important to ensure that everything coming out of our mouths was meant to edify, encourage, and comfort above all things. It all needed to flow through a filter of love. While we cared for the practical needs of the community, we also sought to express God's love through praying for people when they were receptive to it. Sometimes they were physically healed; sometimes they were touched by the words we spoke. Our leaders taught us that God *always* wants to express His love, and for me that concept was life-changing.

I admit, it sounds like butterflies and unicorns. I'll also admit that we made a lot of mistakes. Even today the school is often criticized for the overzealous attempts at ministering by the less tactful students. We were all young, and it was often messy. Yet our leaders explained that our main mission was to present solutions in God's love—not division. The Church needs to show the world how God can help you rather than how He'll punish you. It needs to tear walls down instead of building them up. Living with that mindset wasn't always easy, because it's not the sort of philosophy a lot of us grew up with. But the pastor always said that church can be compared to childbirth: It can be painful and messy and take a lot of pushing, but in the end, that's how you create life.

Another aspect of school that was amazingly beneficial was the new relationships I was able to forge. I spent nine months in a room with seventy other like-minded people of all ages. For a person that had grown up in an environment with very few Christian friends, it was Heaven on Earth.

For the first few months of school we would take a little time per day to highlight one student who would talk about their story and how they came to know God. One guy's story was so close to mine that it shocked me. Slade had been attracted to men for most of his life and had worked through it in recent years. After that day we were able to relate to each other's hardships and encourage each other. He's still a very close and trusted friend.

For the first time in my life I felt like I was really making it. I felt like I was truly doing what God wanted, and even fitting into a group. I was being challenged constantly, but I could actually feel myself growing. It was everything my heart had been crying for.

I was stretched outside of school as well, and in ways that were less welcome at the time but no less important. A month or so after school started I found a job working with the elderly and people with special needs. With one of the most aggressive gag reflexes on the planet, I only took the job on the condition that I wouldn't have to address any "personal needs." My bosses assured me that my position would only include shopping, doing light house cleaning, performing other simple duties for my clients, and that was all.

It could be rewarding at times, and extremely difficult emotionally at others. Some of my clients were sweet, and some would scream at me as I tried to take care of them. And as is usually God's way, I found myself learning in the most unlikely places. In walking out my sobriety I was abstaining from more than just substances; this involved sobriety of my actions and my thought processes as well. I was pulling myself away from destructive thinking and keeping my heart clean along with my body. Because of this, I learned to better appreciate the value of taking care of someone who couldn't take care of themselves. Much of finding God is in humility, and in putting the focus on others rather than myself, I gained a new perspective. These people could hardly accomplish anything on their own and sometimes weren't even able to thank me for my help, and because of it, I gained a new level of compassion and empathy that I had never experienced.

Eventually my bosses sat me down and told me that I was doing a great job, and that they wanted to move me up in the company. I would be required to carry a pager and be on call to help new employees. I would also need to work with a few people who needed "just a tad more personal care." I was assured that it would still be super easy—just a continuation of what I had already been doing. I was so excited by the promotion and the new responsibility that I didn't take long enough to consider what "a tad more personal care" might actually mean.

My first overnight shift in the new position was with a woman with severe multiple sclerosis who was in her mid-forties. She had very little control of her body and was confined to a wheelchair, so seeing her for the first time was a bit overwhelming for me. Walking into the apartment I smiled and greeted her, trying to ignore the sense of unease growing in my stomach.

The girl who usually worked with her walked me through the nightly routine. "Okay, so it's super easy here. Veronica is very sweet. She's hard to understand, so you'll have to be patient with her. You'll feed her dinner at six, give her a shower, and help her into bed around nine. Then you can sleep. She'll call out to you if she needs help in the night. Usually she sleeps until seven." She gave me a checklist and showed me a few more things, then was off. I was nervous, but remained confident in myself.

As I followed the routine I started to notice that Veronica seemed sad. She barely ate any of the broccoli I tried to spoon into her mouth. Her eyes were in her lap most of the time. Thinking that maybe the transition to a new helper was intimidating to her, I tried to lighten the mood with any little jokes I could think of. I was still new to the position and wasn't used to her speech impairment, so I couldn't think of anything to do but put on her favorite show and reassure her the best I could. The night came to a close, and after very proudly being able to give her a shower without any problems, I helped her into bed. In her raspy, slurred voice she said, "Thank you."

I got into my bed in the guest room and pulled the covers over myself, incredibly relieved to finally relax. I thought to myself, *This is great. This is no problem at all. I can totally do this. Good times.* I turned over to get more comfortable, and as I always did before falling asleep, I prayed. Praying had been especially important in recent weeks because I had an important decision to make.

Every student in MA takes an out-of-country mission trip during the summer to do volunteer work and preach the gospel to people from other nations. Mine was still a ways off, but such a big trip takes a lot of planning and financing, so I needed to decide where I was going soon. I had several different choices: Ireland, Africa, and Mexico were a few of the more popular ones. Since I'd never been out of the country before, Ireland was currently at the top of my list. I figured that a nice, First World European country would be a great way to ease myself into such trips, and then during my second year of MA I could go somewhere slightly more challenging. I was talking to God about it when I heard a noise from the other room.

I don't need to describe it, because we all know the sound of projectile vomiting when we hear it. I think it's ingrained in us.

There was a moment when I was so terrified that my mind simply refused to believe what was happening. I pulled the covers over my head, telling myself that it had been nothing more than a half-asleep auditory hallucination. Yeah, I had those all the time. We all do, right? You're falling asleep and you think you hear something, so you jerk awake to find that it had been nothing at all—that your disabled client had not, in fact, just lost her dinner all over the place in the other room with you being the only person available to clean it up.

It wasn't long before the awful reality set in and I ran to Veronica's room. She was lying there, looking miserable. "Oh, sweetie, hold on and let me grab some stuff to clean you up!" I ran to get gloves and towels, trying my best to breathe through my mouth. I came back and cleaned her up, gave her a fresh change of clothes, and stripped all the blankets and sheets. All the while I was holding back my own dinner.

Veronica whispered "I'm sorry," and I felt terrible for gagging; I didn't want her to feel guilty on top of already feeling ill.

"Oh my gosh, Veronica, you have nothing to be sorry about. I just have a weak stomach." I smiled at her and focused everything I had into getting all of it up. When I was finally done I tucked her back into bed. "It makes sense now that you weren't hungry," I said, trying to sound as lighthearted as possible. She nodded up at me.

After I was safely out of the room, I released the meltdown that I'd been holding inside of me for the last half hour. I called my supervisor, freaked out and crying and trying to be as quiet as possible, and told her what happened.

"I can't do this! You said it was going to be easy! She's throwing up! Can you please come and help me with this?" I pleaded with her. But it was no good.

"Sorry Liz, I can't leave my client, and everyone else is working now. You're going to have to deal with it." Her tone was sympathetic, yet direct. "Just think," she added before hanging up, "now you've done it. You've faced your fear of doing something like this and you got through it. Now everything else is going to be cake."

She hung up and I returned to my room. Eventually I managed to calm down, and slumping back into bed I even started to see it from her perspective. *Yeah. That was horrible, but now everything's cool. Now I'll be able to handle anything. I've already experienced the worst of it. It's like ripping off a band-aid.* Finally feeling close to sleep again, I continued to talk with God about my trip.

An image of hundreds of black children in tattered clothes flashed across my mind. For a moment I tried to deny what I'd seen, and then I tried to argue it. "There are poor black children in Ireland," I said defensively.

A kind voice responded, "But not many, Elizabeth."

I was having a hard time wrapping my brain around the very idea of going somewhere like Mozambique, Africa, one of the poorest nations in the world. The idea that God might be currently telling me to go there was even harder to accept. Deep down I knew what was happening, but the reality of it was so hard to take that I literally tried to pretend otherwise. A little like a kid covering her eyes, I thought if I denied it long enough it would just disappear.

The sound of vomiting came again from the other room. This time I couldn't deny it for even a moment. I did however have time to reflect on this occurrence:

Dear God in Heaven! What is happening? What is happening to my life?! Forget all the salvation and healing and growing; the sound of that woman throwing up a second time made my entire world crumble. This was officially the end.

Somehow I managed to gag my way into her room and get her re-cleaned up, and eventually she fell back asleep. I was exhausted by then and decided to sleep on the couch so I could be closer in case it happened again. And it did. I know that she threw up at least five times throughout the night, though by the end I lost count. Being up the entire night, I had a lot of time to work out my grievances with God and His decision regarding my mission trip. Finally I had to admit that this truly was a time of new strength and growth in my life. Feeling like nothing could be as bad as what I was experiencing that night, I conceded.

    I would go to Africa.

seventeen

Batteries in Africa

I began working extra shifts, and I sent out support letters to my friends and family, asking for them to invest in my trip. Everything was locked in now; I would be going to a large orphanage in the heart of Mozambique, and the trip would take close to two weeks. Now all I needed was the funding.

Even with the extra work I managed a few days off one weekend and drove to Wilsonville so I could see everyone before my trip. My first stop was to see Dad and Jackie, and as I've mentioned was common those days, we ate Chinese food. We sat at the table, and as I was dishing out the chow mein onto our plates I noticed a cane leaning up against Dad's recliner.

"Dad, is that yours?" I asked. "Why didn't you tell me you needed a cane now?"

"Oh, I don't use it all the time," he said, trying to be dismissive. "Sometimes it just helps when the pain gets to be a bit too much."

A few months earlier he had started to feel a strange pain in his thigh, and had developed a limp because of it. When it didn't seem to be going away he saw his doctor, but was told that it was just his weight and diabetes. When it kept getting worse, they sent him to a physical therapist, which for the time being had brought him nothing but a lot more pain.

When Dad could see that his casual tone hadn't assuaged my worry, he went on: "Next week your grandparents are going to leave to come out here for a month or so. Just to take off some of the strain while I heal up. I didn't want to worry you; it's really no big deal."

The idea of his leg hurting enough to require the use of a cane was already pretty worrisome, but I trusted his words and moved my thoughts back to the trip. After a fiercely competitive video game session with Jackie I headed out to see friends. And after Dad and Jackie, Jasmine and Lynn were next on the list.

You might have wondered whether my encounter with God and the other dramatic changes in my life had put a strain on my relationships with them, but absolutely nothing changed between us. My beliefs had been altered drastically since we first became close, but that never stopped Jasmine and Lynn from being a continual source of support, and I cannot stress enough just how necessary that was during this time in my life.

Lynn and I met for coffee. When you think of "meeting for coffee" you probably think of sitting down in a Starbucks or similar café, but in Wilsonville that meant getting a coffee from the dispenser at the liquor store and sitting outside with it. We sat ourselves on a bench in the sun, and as soon as we did, Lynn pulled an envelope out of her purse.

"It's not much, Lizzie," she said, "but I wanted to give you something for your trip."

It caught me completely off guard. She knew that the trip was for MA, and probably had some idea that it would involve Christian outreach. Yet she was still willing to donate, and that gesture was powerful to me. I hugged her and thanked her profusely.

As with my tuition, I hadn't known where the money would come from. This time, however, I barely even had time to worry; between the support I'd already received, the money I'd made working extra shifts, and Lynn's donation, all the costs of the trip were basically covered. It was really happening.

And in the blink of an eye, it was time to leave. Our team of eight met for lunch the day before our big adventure began. We ate sushi and talked about our supplies list. It was August, and Sequoia tends to get very hot during the summer—well over a hundred degrees, often over a hundred ten— but we had heard that the weather in Mozambique was tropical and quite mild, so we were looking forward to escaping the heat.

Our trip leader gave us the low-down: "Just remember that if your bag is picked in Customs to be searched, they can confiscate anything. They'll literally steal it if they want it. So distribute things like batteries and food throughout your pack. Also, ladies, don't forget that your legs have to be wrapped in a sarong at all times, even when we're inside the orphanage. No low-cut tops. And guys, you need to bring pants for Sunday church. We're going there to serve their culture, so we need to respect it fully."

She continued as she ate, and the more she spoke the more it began to hit me that I was leaving for Africa in less than twenty-four hours. There was simply no backing out now. This was really happening. The rest of the group chatted and laughed like excited little birds while I sat quietly, poking my California roll with my chopsticks and trying not to poop myself.

It being my first trip out of the country, to say I over-packed was an understatement. I went out and bought a huge hiking pack that was just about as tall as I was, and I must have stuffed a million changes of clothes in there. Most important however, were the flashlights and batteries.

You see, I might have been twenty-two, but I, er, still *on occasion* *cough* slept with a nightlight. Since a very young age night terrors had been common for me. I would often wake up in the middle of the night, sometimes screaming or walking around my room, often not even remembering the whole ordeal the next morning. After a few sleepovers my friends tended to treat me like a werewolf. This trip triggered all sorts of sleep-related anxiety, much of which was due to my simple fear of the dark. And to be completely honest, I was a little afraid of getting my head chopped off in the bush. Our plan was to stay at the large orphanage and travel out on smaller trips while we were there, sometimes sleeping in tents. I'd been camping a handful of times in my life, though my family would probably be considered the *indoorsy* type. As with many aspects of this trip, I would be stretched.

So I went out and bought one of those big boxes of AA batteries from Costco and distributed them throughout my bag: a few at the bottom of my sleeping bag, a few wrapped up in my underwear, a few rolled into my socks, etc. My teammates poked fun at me for it, but there was no way I was spending one second in Africa without access to a flashlight and fresh batteries.

There was another aspect of the trip that was a source of anxiety but also of excitement: I was what my generation would call "mad crushing" on one of the guys in my group.

I had held onto the nun mentality for a while, but over time God began to speak to me in the area of my sexuality, and gradually my heart began to change. The attraction to women was still there, but I acknowledged the attraction to men that was resurfacing. Unfortunately though, instead of coming at it with a fresh outlook and new confidence, I reverted to my days of schoolgirl crushes and mentalities. I lacked the ability to develop male friendships that could later lead to romantic relationships, and instead obsessed over the idea of being pursued.

The next morning came and we all hopped on a plane. The total travel time was about twenty-four hours. We tried sleeping in empty rows when we were afforded them, but it was hard not being able to stretch our legs. Multiple times I snuck into the wide area in the back of the plane and lay on the floor until being woken by the stewardess. I hadn't been familiar with the "kick awake" method until that trip, but I supposed there were different standards on international flights. Finally I discovered that if I put the baby-changing table down in the bathroom I could sit on the sink and extend my legs, so that at least I could stretch them out.

After our grueling series of flights we had to go through Customs. We sent our bags through, and I held my breath.

My bag was the only one chosen to be searched.

We all tried to act cool as they went through it. In the end I'm pretty sure it was my underwear that saved me. I sort of lied earlier about not adopting any of the nun outfit, because those Customs guys found a big pair of granny panties right at the top of the bag, and I guess they decided they'd seen enough.

Stepping outside and seeing that we were truly in Africa was a surreal experience. The jet lag and overall lack of sleep were enough to put a horse down. A small truck arrived and we all squeezed in and headed for the orphanage. During the ride I was very happy to be the thinnest I'd been since I was twelve.

The orphanage was way bigger than I had expected. We were greeted by hundreds of little children in braids, all smiling and pulling at us as we arrived. Lunch was just being served, and the ministry wasn't only feeding the kids; sometimes up to two thousand people were fed every day. The kids sang and danced as they waited in line, and they held our hands as we waited ourselves. These children were often found abandoned in the streets, sometimes left to die in garbage bins as newborns. There was a building on the grounds solely for nursing HIV-positive babies. The leader of the ministry told us that sometimes God healed them and sometimes He took them, but the orphanage's commitment to taking in every single child that was brought to them was unwavering. Right away my heart was overwhelmed.

In addition to visiting the kids we helped out at a small church in the middle of a very arid region. Each night people came from miles around to cram themselves into the little shack and hear us teach about God's love and salvation by candlelight. We prayed for people into the late hours of the night and danced with them as we sang songs to God. The vibrancy of their culture was something I could have never truly appreciated without seeing it firsthand, and their passion amid so many hardships and in such an inhospitable environment was humbling. As with my job caring for the infirm, it really made me realize what I had.

Everywhere we went we saw unbelievable poverty. It lined the streets we drove past. There was a whole city that was built on a garbage dump. And the culture was so foreign to me that sometimes it was a lot to take in all at once. In busier places the cars drove willy-nilly without any sense of order, all blaring their horns at each other. Sometimes we bought and ate mysterious packaged food that we hoped wasn't monkey brains.

One of the biggest issues was water; in some areas there was very little. There was a better supply in the more lush places we visited, but it tasted so bad that we had to mix it with Kool-Aid just to make it a little more tolerable—and of course doing so would then prevent it from fully hydrating us. It's easy to take something like water for granted, but when you're forced to choke down brown, grape-flavored water in order to stay alive, it really puts things like faucets and showers and swimming pools into perspective.

One evening we piled into the flatbed truck and were taken on a few-hour drive to our next destination. It was cold, so we all brought our sleeping bags and blankets. There were so many of us that we were jammed together, and I was afforded the opportunity that every sparkly-eyed girl dreams of: I was seated next to my crush, and due to the lack of room he even offered to let me lay my head on his arm. Oh, the magic in the air! We talked for a few hours as the truck brought us down the dark road. It was the first time I thought that maybe he liked me back—that maybe I wasn't just imagining it.

On another night we were driving to our next destination when the truck stopped. The driver told us that we were to get out and walk the rest of the way. No one was sure why this was happening, including our guide, but we got out anyway and the truck drove off. We weren't far from where we were going, but the sun was setting rapidly. On top of that, we were in the woods. Everyone looked worried as we set off, following the guide. Very soon it was pitch black.

This was the perfect recipe for a panic attack. I was on the other side of the world, as far away as possible from all my friends and family. I was marching through the African wilderness in the dead of night. Even the leaders of our group, who I always looked to for strength, were grabbing each other's shirts and whispering about lions with the rest of the team. We could hear drums in the distance. And despite my commitment to always being prepared, I didn't have a flashlight on me. None of us did. It was a terrifying situation.

And yet, in the unlikeliest of places, I found that fear was far from me. There are times in my life when I believe one thing yet feel another—when I know that I'm where God wants me to be, yet it doesn't stop me from worrying or being afraid. But on that dark road I felt more than ever the rightness in what I was doing. Sometimes it's hard to identify exactly what God wants for us, but every footstep through those trees was perfectly in line with the path He had set for me. And because of this, I was completely certain that we were safe. It was one of the most liberating experiences of my life.

A few days before we were set to leave our leaders arranged for a short car safari and a few nights in a motel, so we could unwind and talk about what we'd experienced. We saw giraffes, zebras, lions and wild pigs, though unfortunately the wildlife back at the café proved to be hostile. Monkeys made every attempt possible to steal our stuff and grab our empty plates, and no one could open up a can of soda without a swarm of bees crawling inside!

Growing progressively more excited to take a good shower and sleep in a bedroom, I decided to surprise Dad with a phone call. I broke away from the group and found a payphone, and when Dad answered I yelled, "Hi, it's me, Dad!"

"Hi, Gayle. How's your trip?" Despite hearing from me for the first time in nearly two weeks, he sounded very down. I gave him some quick details and told him when I would be back, sensing all the while that something was wrong. Grandma was waiting to talk to me, so Dad quickly passed off the phone and she filled me in.

"Things are real hard here, Elizabeth. Your grandfather and I are doing all we can. Your dad can barely walk. We've been to the doctor and they keep sending him home, saying it's his diabetes. I feel like they're missing something, because he's just getting worse." Her tone had grown heavy. Tears filled my eyes as I listened, and my heart reached helplessly for the other side of the planet.

～ eighteen ～

People in the Hallway

Once I arrived back in the States I still had a few days before I had to return to work. I'd originally planned to spend it at my apartment, unwinding and thinking on my adventure, but instead I rushed back to Wilsonville. The mood there was heavy and somber. My dad lay in bed much of the time, in terrible pain. Depression was settling over the household, and it didn't take much exposure before I was caught up in it as well. A strong feeling of hopelessness held each of us—a feeling that, due to the doctors' complete unwillingness to run any real tests or even admit that there might be a serious problem, had an almost nightmarish quality.

Adding heavily to this surreality, the household was woken up early one morning by one of the women from the church. She told us to turn on the news—that America was under attack. We turned on the TV and found footage of two planes crashing into the World Trade Center on every channel. Now the confusion and hopelessness that we were all experiencing covered the entire nation. It felt like some awful dream that I just couldn't wake up from. And all of this only a week or so after returning home from Africa.

I was reluctant to drive home and return to work, but once again my dad assured me that my grandparents could take care of everything and bring him to his appointments.

One perk to going home, however, was that I was able to spend time with my new roommate. Heading into my second year of MA I'd needed someone to share the two-bedroom apartment with, and Amber and I fast became friends when she moved in shortly before my leaving for Africa. Having a roommate who was a Christian and who also shared my sense of humor helped ease the pain of being away from my family.

One night, shortly after returning to Sequoia, my mind was flooded with vivid dreams that were filled with happiness and hope. Mentors I admired and great people of faith visited me and encouraged me throughout the night. I woke up in a joyful mood and started making breakfast, basking in this rejuvenated atmosphere. It was almost tangible. Amber came into the kitchen and sat at the table, and I asked her if she wanted some eggs.

"Nah, I'm alright," she said. "When did Joel leave?"

"Joel?" I looked at her curiously. "What do you mean?" Joel was a good friend of ours, but we never hung out alone, and certainly not in my room.

"Yeah, I heard Joel in your room with you earlier this morning. Well, I thought it was Joel. It was a man's voice." I dropped my spatula and sat down, and she continued, clearly picking up on the fact that something was weird here: "You guys were laughing together! It sounded like you were having a great time! That wasn't Joel? Who was it?"

Chills ran down my arms. "I had incredible dreams last night. No one was in the room with me." We both looked at each other wide-eyed. Apparently *incredible* didn't quite cover it.

Two weeks after that night I received a call from my Grandma. "Elizabeth, your dad was airlifted to the hospital in the city. He was in a coma, but he's awake now. They're going to run tests there. You need to come now." There was an urgency in her voice that scared me.

It was all I could do to keep myself calm during the agonizing four-hour drive. As soon as I got there Grandma brought me to see the doctor. I sat in his office and he told me what was going on:

"We ran some tests on your father, and cancer has spread throughout his entire body. It looks like it might have originated in his prostate. We're not sure why none of his other doctors caught this, since it's so advanced. We don't know how long he has to live. It may only be a few weeks. We can make him as comfortable as possible."

Comfortable. The word rang in my ears. It had only been three years since I'd heard it last in this context, and here I was again, struggling with the reality of it all. The first time it had been painful to hear, but this time my mind just sort of froze, dazed.

Grandma put her arm around mine as we left the office. "Grandma, I think I need to run back home and grab my things so I can stay here as long as I can. I don't want to miss any more time. I'll go and come back in the morning, and I think I'll take Jackie—get him out of here for a while." She agreed.

Composing myself, I walked into Dad's hospital room. We were alone at the moment, and the TV was blaring. Dad was in a gown, hooked up to an I.V., and looking more sick and vulnerable than I'd ever seen him. All I could think to say was, "Hey, Dad. I heard you went on a helicopter ride."

Dad wasn't looking at me. He seemed disoriented. "I didn't like it because of the oxygen mask, and being strapped down. I felt claustrophobic." He pointed past me. "Do you see those people in the hall?"

I turned, and my heart sank when I saw that the hall was empty. He was on pain meds, but I knew that wasn't enough to explain this. "No, Dad. There's no one there."

"Oh, okay," he said pretty casually. "They said I'm seeing things that aren't there. Is this real?" He touched his index finger to a point on his blanket.

"It's your blanket, Dad. There's nothing on it." I fought back tears. The urge to get going was incredibly strong now. I needed to get to Sequoia and back as soon as possible, and to ask my school leaders to pray for his healing.

"Are you sure?" he asked. "It looks like there's something on my blanket." He moved his finger over the spot, as though trying to feel whatever it was.

The next moment still lives vividly in my mind. For some reason I made the very deliberate choice not to say goodbye to him. I just told him that I loved him, and that I would see him the next day. Then I left to find Jackie.

We made good time until we were stopped for road construction just before the spot where the winding mountain pass hits the freeway. Jackie and I waited for traffic to move, both of us trying to cope minute-by-minute. In times like these everything can either bounce off of your dazed mind or it can strike you with a vividness and intensity that stays with you forever, and this was the latter. The sun and the mountain scenery overtook my heart. The grandness of the landscape brought peace and hope, and the knowledge that God was present.

As soon as we arrived in town I met with some of my leaders at the church. They prayed for me and for Dad's healing, and told me that Pastor John (our senior pastor) would go to pray for my Dad himself once he was back from his trip. In such a large and busy church, this encouragement and generosity filled me with joy and renewed my faith that Dad would soon be healed by God. By then it was getting late, so Jackie and I went to visit with some of my friends at their house. We ate dinner and chatted, and for just a little while we were able to unwind and forget about the craziness and the uncertainty.

Around ten o'clock in the evening an inexplicable wave of God's presence came over me. I picked up my cell phone and called my friend Peter to fill him in on the latest updates and ask him to pray. As we spoke I said, "It's the weirdest thing, Peter, but all of a sudden I just feel such a great presence of joy. It feels like Christmas! I don't know how to explain it!" Right then I heard my call-waiting signal and told him I would call him back.

I answered, and the last thing I expected to hear was my grandpa's voice. Grandma was usually the phone person.

"Elizabeth, I don't know how to tell you this, but your dad just died." His voice cracked as he spoke.

Without skipping a beat I said, "Don't move the body, we're on our way! I love you Grandpa, and I'm sorry I'm not there." I hung up the phone, completely certain that this wasn't Dad's time to die. If there was one thing I'd learned in MA it was that Jesus healed the sick, cast out demons, and raised the dead.

I made some phone calls and in short order Jackie and I, my friend and her daughter, Peter and his friend Tim, and Amber packed into two cars and headed for the hospital. It was late, and this would be the third time I'd made this drive in one day, but I was energized and feeding on the collective belief that my Dad would be brought back. On the way there I prayed and thought about what would happen when he was raised from the dead. What the nurses might do when it happened, what the doctors might say, what the newspaper the next day might read. I'd seen stranger miracles documented, so why could it not happen for our family?

We arrived around three in the morning and some of our group stayed in the waiting room while Peter, Tim and I went straight to Dad. Katherine was there, and knowing what was about to happen, she brought my grandparents out of the room. They might not have approved of what we were going to do, or even understood it. Fortunately they thought my friends were people from the morgue and went to rest, which made me glad. They had stood watch over my dad for so long, and if anyone needed some time, it was them.

What happened next was sort of a blur, like a strange dream. We prayed over Dad, commanded his spirit to be returned to his body. I remember being amazed by the look on his face: smiling and peaceful, as though he caught a glimpse of something wonderful as he passed. The guys were speaking in tongues, and at one point I'm pretty sure I was standing up on a chair—things that now, normally, would make me feel very uncomfortable. The nurse had to keep coming in to tell us to keep it down. I feel bad that we put her through so much, but at the time I remember looking into her eyes with sincerity and respect and saying, "You only get one father. I'm going to fight for mine."

Hours went by as we prayed fiercely for Dad's return. At times it felt as though I were actually arguing with him to come back. Tim, who didn't even know my father or anything about him, said, "Jack, you are not a failure. Get back into your body."

In the early hours of the morning there finally came a time when I needed a short rest if I was to continue at all. Peter and Tim stayed with Dad and I joined Jackie and my friends in the waiting room. I lay down on a couple of chairs, but I couldn't sleep. As the sun started to peak over the mountains I decided I should charge my phone in case any of my teachers called. I went out to the car and plugged it into the cigarette lighter, and right as I did so it started to ring. When I picked it up I found Pastor John on the line.

"Tell me what's happening," he said. The gratitude I felt nearly floored me. This man pastored a church of over a thousand and traveled all over the world. For him to call me, at this hour, was huge. I knew when we started the conversation that God would speak through him.

I filled him in on everything that had happened, and when I was done he said, "I don't have a clear word for you."

There was a moment of silence, and I became frustrated. I thought to myself, *He doesn't have a clear word? What does that even mean? If anyone's going to get a clear word it's going to be him, right?*

Finally he said, "Well let me ask you a question: Does he want to come back?"

And right then it was as though someone were truly telling me that Dad had died for the first time. Suddenly, the fact that he'd given up all hope and purpose in life since Mom's death was very clear, and I knew that the will was a very powerful thing. The tension of the situation dissipated all at once, and the realization that he was really gone threatened to overwhelm me. Not sure what to do or say, I blurted out, "My brother is going to need to go to the church's high school."

"We can arrange that," Pastor John said calmly.

Just then, Peter and Tim came walking up to the car. It was the first time they'd left my dad's side since we arrived. Pastor John asked to speak with Tim, and I handed the phone over to him. Peter's eyes were very sad as he spoke to me. "God just told us to stop praying. So we came to find you."

We walked back up to the waiting room, and everyone could tell by the looks on our faces that we were done. The hospital chaplain came and asked us if she could say a prayer over Dad before they took his body. My grandparents, Jackie and I went into his room and stood around the bed while she read a prayer. I held Jackie, who was two days shy of his fourteenth birthday, and we wept as we said goodbye.

Katherine drove us back to Wilsonville, and I stared out the window as the grieving process started all over again. There were a lot of decisions to be made in the coming weeks, but in my mind the biggest question had only one answer: My brother was coming to live with me. Our grandparents were elderly and lived in Oklahoma. Everyone later agreed that Sequoia was the best choice.

Pulling into the church parking lot we were amazed by what we saw. The marquee in front of the elementary school read, "*THOMAS*

FAMILY — OUR THOUGHTS ARE WITH YOU." I had no idea how anyone from the school could have possibly heard already.

And so we began the long and arduous process of preparing for the funeral and moving everything out of the home I'd known since I was seven, and the *only* home Jackie had ever known. Pulling ourselves away from the house and watching as much of Mom and Dad's stuff was sold was heart-wrenching, and at times surreal. I was blessed to have my grandparents there to help, as they're famous for their precision, efficiency, and their packing and moving abilities, which borderline on superhuman.

The week Dad died I went home for a few days to put some things in order and talk to my teachers about what the next season looked like for me. They urged me to continue my second year of MA and work at a pace that I could handle. It was hard to be around large groups of people while I was still actively grieving, but that Sunday I forced myself to go to church anyway.

Before he began his message, Pastor John gave a testimony he had heard earlier that week. It wasn't even from our church, but we were big on sharing testimonies from all places and denominations. Hearing about the goodness of God builds faith, regardless of who's telling it or where.

"We heard a report that a nurse in Minnesota was attending to a baby who died during delivery. After failed attempts to resuscitate, the parents said goodbye, and she took the child's body away so that it could be prepared for the morgue. Her heart ached as she held this baby, and something rose up inside herself, willing her to pray. She spoke life over the body, and at that moment the child returned to life."

The congregation erupted in cheers. I sat there numb, just waiting for the service to be over, when God spoke softly to my heart: "Your prayers were not wasted. Nothing is wasted in My kingdom."

When Mom died, there was a massive outpouring of support from the community. When Dad died, it was tripled.

We drove to the church in the nearby town, which was much larger than our own. The place was absolutely packed with friends, family, and people from around town who had nothing to do with our church and who only knew Dad as a passing acquaintance, yet still felt impacted by him. His funeral was like a huge public event; it was remarkable, to say the least. As he had with Mom's funeral, Dad's best friend led the procession. If there was anyone outside of our own family who was impacted as heavily by the death, it was him, and yet he led with strength and his own beautiful words. A mighty man of God.

Near the end I invited anyone who wanted to say something about Dad up to the front. One sweet girl in her teens took the microphone and cried as she spoke. She apologized for crying, and I told her exactly what Dad would have said: "Well you know, it's a funeral. It *is* allowed." That got a big laugh and helped lighten the mood, and I knew Dad would have wanted it that way.

At one point there was a short silence as we all waited for anyone else who wanted to speak. It was broken when my high school band teacher stood up. This man—this old rocker hippie whose band opened for Jefferson Starship in the seventies—stood up spontaneously and performed an acapella rendition of *Amazing Grace*, eyes closed, swaying slightly as he sang.

My father died on October 16th, 2001 at the age of forty-six—three years after the death of our mother. I was twenty-two and my brother was thirteen.

～ nineteen ～

Out of the Limelight

It's incredible how so much can change in so little time. Amber graciously moved out after living with me for only three months, and Jackie moved in. We were assigned to a social worker and filed the proper paperwork to make me his legal guardian. I enrolled him in the church's high school program, which worked with a charter school to give him the social, educational, and even spiritual dynamics he needed. He took this new chapter in life as an opportunity to finally make the jump from *Jackie* to *Jack*, though I'm not sure if I'll ever fully acclimate to that change.

With my emotional state as it was and with my new responsibilities, I didn't think I could care for the infirm anymore, so my gracious bosses hired me to clean their offices and a few houses—and for much more than a housecleaner would normally get. I can still remember the look on Jack's face when I burst into the house, absolutely ecstatic, and told him that he would be helping me clean houses at my amazing new blessing-of-a-job. He just sort of looked at me, wondering how being doomed to clean houses was cause for celebration.

Finally, with everything set, Jackie and I went about living this new life. I told myself that I was no longer just the sister, but the *sistermother*, whose purpose was not to torture—as siblings can do by God-given right—but to nurture. At least, that was the idea. But when you're in your early twenties and you're tasked with raising your fourteen-year-old brother, there's an odd dynamic involved. I often had to pull rank and force him to do his homework or take a shower (that kid would go weeks without bathing if you didn't say anything), but no matter what, we were still brother and sister. It was also an odd time; at times it felt as though Mom and Dad were out of town and we had the house all to ourselves, and at others we felt alone and were filled with grief. We stayed up late and ate ice cream while we watched Star Trek. We fought over school work and household chores. We laughed our butts off at dumb inside jokes. We went at each other's throats like rabid dogs while we cleaned houses. We cried together when the grief became too much. We were a young woman trying to find herself and make it through life, and a stubborn teen trying to adjust to a new and very different world. There are times when I regret that I couldn't have been a more solid parental figure for him, but then I remember that I was struggling with the lack of a father and mother just as much as he was. Things were never perfect, and there are many things I would do differently if given the chance, but this was an important time in both of our lives. It bonded us together, closer than if things had turned out the way they were "supposed to."

School was difficult during this time, and I lagged behind in my bookwork, but my leaders constantly encouraged me to keep going. The smaller second-year class made it easier to make and maintain relationships, and the support I received from my classmates was invaluable. I still had feelings for Mr. Crush, and I tried to ignore them for a while. Now whatever happened in my romantic life would ultimately affect Jack, so I thought it best to put it all out of my mind. Finally though, under the advice of a friend, I cracked and told Mr. Crush how I felt. He told me he wasn't ready to date. It was the classic out, especially in the Church. Today I thank God for the plans He would later have for me, but at the time this was very hard. Being single started to feel like it was my cross to bear, and every month that went by without so much as a romantic lead grew more and more painful.

Things were hard, but as He always has, God placed people in my life to provide comfort and guidance. The Denvers, a family from church that I had come to know shortly before Dad died, became like my second family. Diane and Donald helped fill the parental void in my heart, and gave us everything from meals to shoulders to cry on. Sometimes they would offer advice, and other times they would do exactly what most grieving people want: nothing at all. If you've ever lost a loved one, it's likely that you'll know what I mean when I say that sometimes you just want someone to be with you while you cry. After one particularly bad episode, Donald sat with me for as long as I needed. When I finally calmed down he just looked at me and said, "You want to go to Walmart with me?" And I did want to go. Somehow that was *exactly* what I wanted. It was such a simple thing, and you might laugh at the idea, but often all you can do with grief is see it through. Sometimes all your heart needs is companionship.

If there was anyone that truly felt like my adopted mother however, it was Katherine. She had been so close to Mom that spending time with her almost felt a little like being with Mom herself. And I spent as much time with her as I could, especially in those early days. Any weekend we could manage, Jack and I made the trip back to Wilsonville where he would stay with one of his friends, I would visit Jasmine and Lynn, and both of us would spend a few days at Katherine and her husband Ron's house. These trips were our way of staying connected with our old town, or at least of feeling the occasional bit of nostalgia that made us feel less homesick. Katherine's house in particular felt like our home away from home; the little place, tucked into the woods, had been there for most of my life and all of Jack's. Staying there felt both like a return home and an escape from everyday stresses. Just like with the Denvers, I don't know what I would have done if I didn't have Katherine's love and support during this time.

Finishing up my second year of MA was difficult, but rewarding. After it was over, however, my life began to lose focus.

I returned to junior college in an attempt to finish my degree and found that school was more difficult than before. I gravitated toward art classes, which caused me to lag in other areas. In retrospect, I probably should have just gone for a degree in art. After I was done with school I figured I should learn a trade that could make me money regardless of what else I was doing in life, so I took classes to become a certified massage therapist. I enjoyed helping people, and multiple jobs opened up because of my skill, which certainly helped our financial situation…yet as time went on I still found myself feeling more and more lost in life as a whole.

While raising Jackie could be difficult—he was now taller than me, skinny as a rail despite eating like a pig, as stubborn and contrary as teens come—it was the responsibility itself that weighed me down.

Between being a mom before I was ready, a lack of romantic relationships, and not having any real goals in life, I began to feel a growing disconnect between myself and my peers. My MA friends all seemed to still have that fire of God roaring in their hearts, and they all passionately pursued their dreams, whether through a career in ministry or something outside the Church. Everyone around me seemed to be so full of life that it became progressively more difficult to be around them. Just a few years previous I had related to them all, had laughed and worshipped God with them. Now I felt like the group I'd been so happy to gain admittance to had moved on without me. I tried to remain faithful and to keep walking in freedom, but I couldn't help but feel an awful sense of déjà vu.

I had truly met the Lord. I had come to know Him closely, and had given up the physical vices that bogged me down. I had faced my rejection, cast off lies about myself, and integrated into a congregation that accepted and loved me. I had gone on a grand adventure and learned an incredible amount about myself, about people, and about the world around me. I had embarked on a bold new chapter of my life, with the clouds parting before me as I went. For the first time I'd actually begun to find joy and happiness. As I said before, I'd reached a point where this book should have ended.

But things don't always work that way. Now both of my parents were dead; I was given a great heap of responsibility I would never have expected; my life felt as though it would never go anywhere; and the sense of isolation I thought I had left behind was on me again, reviving the old lies and further weakening my already-strained relationships with the people around me. And with this old pain came the same desires to escape from it. Freedom of the mind is just as important as sobriety of the body, so even though these were only thoughts (I still hadn't been under the influence of drugs or alcohol since returning to God), you could say that I was only staying half-sober. Dwelling on how great it would have felt to get high and forget about everything lent the drug power over me without my even needing to use it. Beginning to believe these lies again was a drug in itself, for self-loathing can be addictive.

On top of everything, I had gained a lot of weight back. Jack and I both sought comfort in food, and while he had clearly inherited Mom's genes, I was still stuck with Dad's. Because of our love of devouring entire boxes of donuts combined with a schedule that made exercise more difficult, I lost the progress I had started making in my senior year of high school. This was the icing on the cake, the cherry on top. Now I was further from loving myself *in addition* to feeling further from my friends, still far from achieving anything worthwhile, and subconsciously allowing my heart to harden toward God. It seems preposterous—impossible, even, considering what He'd done for me—but this is the nature of our hearts. Our relationship with God can affect our relationships with ourselves and with others. Weaken one, and the others will most often weaken as well.

Over time my trips to Wilsonville became more frequent, and more often Jack was staying in Sequoia with a friend when I went. My connections with Jasmine and Lynn and with Katherine were the deepest I had, so I clung to them and sought the comfort of their presence whenever I could. I visited other old friends from high school as well, trying to relive that little sliver of the Good Ol' Days as often as possible. There came a time when I was probably visiting them all *too* much, and the comfort and nostalgia of the visits drifted closer and closer to true escapism.

And on one such trip, made compulsively by myself one day, I took that escapism to a new extreme.

~ twenty ~

One Lost Christian Walks into a Bar...

Seventy-two miles an hour. Fast enough to feel like the four-hour drive was going by more quickly, but not quite fast enough to be pulled over. Five CD's and three bags of gas station candy later (I'm certain at least one of those bags contained Jelly Bellies), I pulled into the long dirt driveway and let myself through the locked gate to Spring's house. This one was made from weather-worn aluminum. In a town like Wilsonville, such gates are as common as mailboxes.

I pulled up to the house and Spring greeted me. "Hey, Liz! How was the drive?"

"It was good," I said, and she gave me a big hug.

We moved around to the garden out back, where we chatted while she finished up. She moved a hose from one tomato plant (we'll call it a tomato plant) to another as she said, "Hey, do you want to go to Shakers tonight? They're having a deal on appetizers."

"Sure, that sounds great," I said. "I'm going to call Katherine and let her know when I'll be there tomorrow." I went inside and pulled out my phone. I had recently upgraded to one with an actual color screen instead of the green and black LCD that made it look like a graphing calculator. Hey, this was the early 2000's, and I needed to get with the times.

Katherine answered with her usual soft "Hello?"

"Hey, Katherine, I'm in town. Me and Spring are going to go..." (I hesitated for a moment) "...*out* tonight. How about I get to your house around lunchtime tomorrow?"

"Okay, dear; that sounds good. I'll have lemon bars waiting." If you've ever heard of the five Love Languages, there's a little-known sixth one, and it's *lemon bars*. Katherine knew this well.

A few hours later we were in the car, and I was checking my wallet to make sure I had enough cash for the chicken wings that were already calling to me from up ahead.

"How's your brother?" Spring asked as she pulled into the parking lot.

"He's good. He's got a friend over, and he's set with enough frozen chimichangas for the weekend."

"He'll be a senior soon, huh?" She pulled into a spot and we got out of the car.

"Yeah, this fall. Gosh..." I imagined myself as a high school senior and marveled at the fact that Jackie was already nearly that old... But as we walked up to Shakers, I pushed it out of my mind.

I had only been inside the building a few times in my life. I was familiar with basically every other business in the community, but

Shakers was always that mysterious building right off the highway that I never dared enter. Mom and Dad hadn't spoken fondly of it, seeing as they had tended to many families with parents who spent a lot of time there, abusing alcohol.

Exhausted from the drive and from the pressures of life, however, the atmosphere in Shakers was very appealing. Being the largest business in town and the only place to grab a beer after work, the place was bustling. It was dark and filled with smoke, music, and raucous laughter—different enough from normal life to be oddly refreshing, especially considering the slightly rebellious spirit that was currently hanging over me. Escape was what I wanted, even if all that meant was a change of scenery.

We sat down at the bar (Spring strategically placing herself next to her current target: a young man named Joey). "Hey Bob, I'll have a Great White," she said to the bartender, and looked at me. "What do you want, Liz? I'm buying."

I looked at the rows of bottles behind the bar, and a tiny war played out inside of me within the span of a few seconds. A Plain Jane sort of angel appeared on my right shoulder. A fat diva devil appeared on my left. They played a quick game of *Rock Paper Scissors* and when the devil won she decided that I would be having a... Well, to be honest, I would forget what she chose after five shots of it.

Before I got the first one—which I adamantly yet very foolishly told myself would be the *only* one—I noticed a guy looking at me from a booth across the room. Spring noticed it too, and turned momentarily from her flirtatious conversation with Joey.

"Liz, that guy's checking you out."

I turned my attention back to the bar. "No way. People don't check me out. He's probably looking for the bathroom." The bartender handed me my drink, and I downed it.

The moment it hit my stomach that fat little diva pressing down on my shoulder ordered another one. Suddenly the pressure on my heart had a place to go. My pain had been in the shadows, waiting to pounce, waiting to break me or to find some sort of release. It was too easy to revert back to my old methods of coping—like slipping on a pair of stinky old sneakers.

Before I took my second shot, Nameless Guy came over. He's nameless because I legitimately don't remember his name. You can make one up.

The conversation went something like, "Blah blah blah blah blah, I like your nails, blah blah blah." During the bit with the nails I looked down at them, remembering that I had painted them the night before. *They* do *look nice, don't they?* I thought to myself, and blushed. The guy could have said that he liked cheese and had a magic outhouse that took him to Jupiter and I would have been just as enamored. A human being of the male persuasion was flirting with me, and that was enough to give me the old schoolgirl butterflies. After a little more of this I had my third shot, and things were loosening up fast.

At one point I excused myself and hopped off the barstool (fell off the barstool), pulling Spring into the bathroom after me. She checked her mascara while I washed my hands nervously.

"He's really into you!" she said. "Are you having fun?"

"Yeah, I'm stoked. But here's the thing." I looked her in the eyes through the reflection of the mirror. "Promise me you won't let me sleep with him. I'm serious." In retrospect it was obviously very silly to insist that my friend keep post over my own morality, but that's what I did.

"Okay, yeah. So Joey and I want to go hang back at my place. Invite Nameless and we'll all be there, so nothing too intense will happen." She finished up with her makeup, threw her arm over my shoulder, and led me back out into the meat market. I finished up my fourth and fifth drinks and we made our way back to Spring's house with Joey and Nameless in tow. We hung out for a few hours, and…

Well, you know the saying, "one thing led to another"? Yeah, I don't think I need to tell you what happened next…

But I will.

Nameless and I had sex.

After the dirty deed was done, I bolted like a scared deer. I straight up threw on my clothes, grabbed my keys, jumped in the car and burned rubber, leaving Nameless behind in a cloud of shame and bad breath.

I had sobered up enough to drive and headed straight for Katherine's house. It was the middle of the night, so during the thirty-minute drive I formulated a plan in which I would park in their yard and sleep in the car until morning. Then I would act like I just got there. It was a foolproof plan. I arrived and parked in the dark driveway, bundling up against the early Spring chill. Trying to get comfortable enough to lie down, I started the car back up so I could run the heat.

There's a scientific law that states that car alarms will only go off when no one is actually breaking into the car, and when they would cause the most disruption and/or annoyance. It's sort of like Murphy's Law. *Whatever car alarm can go off and wake a bunch of people up, will go off and wake a bunch of people up.*

Somehow I managed to trigger that stupid alarm, and I tried desperately to turn it off again. My mind raced, wondering what on Earth I should do. Do I drive off and pretend this never happened? Do I run into the woods, climb a tree and hide? After managing to fumble it off I sat there, frozen in my seat. I held onto the small hope that maybe Katherine and Ron had managed to sleep through it.

A minute later, Katherine ran outside in her nightgown and jacket. I opened the door to meet her.

"What on Earth are you doing out here, sweetie?" Her brows were tightly furrowed in concern.

"I was sick." Yes, brilliant. I'm amazing at making up stories on the fly.

"Why are you in our yard so early? Come inside."

Inside the house Katherine put on some hot water for tea, and I went into the spare room, just off the kitchen. I sat on the bed, trying to compose myself. There was a massive knot in the hair on the back of my head, and as I untangled it the entirety of the night hit me all over again. I breathed deeply, trying to steady myself as I waited for her to join me. I stared at the *Jesus Loves Me* stationary on the nightstand next to the bed. Similar Christian symbols filled her entire home.

When Katherine came in and sat next to me, she clearly knew that something wasn't right. Finally the pressure was too much to bear and I threw myself down beside her, sobbing.

"I did something horrible, Katherine." My words were muffled by the pillow. The fat little diva was pressing my head down into it, cackling.

Katherine put a gentle hand on my back. "Oh, honey. Did you smoke pot?"

"I *wish* I had smoked pot!" I sobbed.

"Well whatever you tell me, I'll still love you." She stroked my back.

Not bearing to hold onto it any longer, I blurted out: "I got drunk and slept with a guy."

Without hesitation she bent down and held me, and she cried too—not in the throes of shame, but because she knew how much I must have been hurting. We held each other and cried, just a pile of sobbing women who loved Jesus.

Always wise and able to think clearly in any situation, she first commanded in the name of Jesus that no pregnancy or disease would result from that night. She prayed for a while, then said gently, "Oh, honey. It's all going to be okay. When I first met the Lord I made all sorts of mistakes." She sat me up and looked into my eyes as I tried to dry my tears. "In my life," she continued, "there have been many things that I knew weren't the best for me, and that I felt like I couldn't break free from. It was only the times that I turned to God and received His love that I was able to do so. No matter what I did, there was never a time when criticism, fear, condemnation, or browbeating ever led me to the truth. Not once. When I believed that His love was based on my actions and ran from Him, I never obtained the grace that I needed to come out on the other side of things. I only found peace when I ran toward Him, when I accepted that He would love me no matter what I did. I realized that even if I were the worst person in the world, He would still love me unconditionally."

As she spoke, I felt weight coming off of me. Tears still streamed down my face, but the little diva was gone. It was as though she were preaching directly to my heart. They tell you God's love is unconditional in Sunday school; you read it in the Bible; you hear it from your pastors.

It's a truth so obvious that it hardly needs to be said, yet it can be nearly impossible for some people to believe—even if they tell themselves that they do. And even after all I'd been through, even after growing so much and spending so much time with God, I realized that in a way I had been one of those people. I had been prepared to condemn myself, possibly for the rest of my life, for what I'd just done. And at this crossroads, where the path split cleanly in two, one side leading toward God in the north and the other leading dead south, Katherine took my arm and guided me in the right direction. And I know that God had put her there, right in the middle of the fork, with a soft smile and an outstretched hand. We talked through the very early morning hours, further processing what had happened, crying, praying.

Was this the happy ending I've been referring to throughout this whole book—the one that every struggling person wishes for? Well, I don't believe such endings are a part of God's plan. No life can be forever without challenges, because to face challenges is to learn, and to learn is to live. No matter where we've gone, there's still more to explore. That night wasn't a *happily ever after*. But it was as close to one as I would ever need.

Like all things, it was the beginning of a new era, a new chapter.

A new journey.

~ twenty-one ~

The Long Journey

As I said, there are no instant fixes when it comes to facing the consequences of our actions, but we can have moments of revelation that lead to healing. I've had multiple such encounters and revelations, but that morning with Katherine brought a deeper understanding of the condition of my life than any I'd experienced before—a deeper realization of who I was and who God is. One of the key elements of this new mindset was repentance, which was something I realized I had been missing. Another was my willingness to open up fully and seek council. Through both, remarkable truths about my life that had remained locked up for decades were revealed. When I brought my sin out of hiding and fully into the light, I was finally able to overcome it.

Everything up to this point has been mostly narrative in nature, but now I'd like to switch gears and give some more practical information and explain my process of repenting, renewing my mind, and receiving wholeness in my life. I'm bringing it all together, here at the end, because it's impossible to put it all on a timeline; it's been like slowly peeling layers off an onion. This is the meat of my experiences—the stuff that would be dog-eared and highlighted in bright yellow before shipping off to my past self.

In the pages to follow you'll find that I refer to "sin." This is a Biblical word that has been used by the greater Christian community to the point of being synonymous with other words like "condemnation" and "evil" and "brimstone" and whatever else you can think of. When taken out of context, talking about sin can seem harsh or accusatory, but when I talk about sin I want to make sure we're using a clear definition of it.

Sin means *to miss the mark*. We're all sinners, because we all miss the mark. The Bible teaches that through Jesus' sacrifice and through our own acceptance of God's love, we have eternal life, which is salvation. Jesus paid the price for our sin so that we could come before God. With that said, I do believe that we are called to gain more than simple entrance into heaven—that salvation is only the starting place of the Christian life.

To truly serve God with holy lives means addressing and facing our sinful nature. Sin causes us to live in a place that we were never created for, therefore robbing us of God's plan for our lives. I do believe that sin makes God unhappy, but not because He's angry that we've broken His rules. He's unhappy because it means we're not living with the gift that He paid a great price for.

Yes, according to the Bible homosexuality is a sin. But so is pride. So is lying. Stealing. Having a lustful thought. These are *all* things that God asks us to address. Repentance is when we accept God's best for us by receiving what He says about sin. Repentance means *to change your mind*. So while sin causes us to miss the mark, repentance is how we move back toward it. This is a concept that you'll see was key in my walk.

twenty-two

Dealing with Grief and Facing Pain

After committing what I perceived as my greatest sin, I was propelled toward God, whereas feelings of condemnation had always propelled me away. Because of this I was able to step back and see where the event stemmed from; I came to realize that I was very vulnerable during that time in my life, and that a lot of it could be attributed to the overwhelming loneliness and unresolved grief I was feeling.

I'm in no way excusing my behavior as anything other than sin. Sin as a means of relieving pain is never compartmentalized; it involves all parts of who we are. I had previously attempted to fix areas of unholiness in my life by my own means, so first I needed to address the overwhelming nature of my circumstances and repent of the mindsets that kept me bound. In order to do this, however, I had to receive God's love and grace for me.

Grief is such a powerful emotion. I liken the intensity of my grief at that time to being in a carnival tilt-o-wheel, being spun around to the point of vomiting while being stabbed repeatedly in the leg by another deranged passenger, then being pushed off the ride by a fat guy smoking a cigar.

During this time of grief (and indeed before it), I based my identity on my weaknesses, and that always led me down a road that separated me from God's purposes. When I saw God as someone who required a certain performance before access to Him could be permitted, I fell back into habits that gave me a false sense of comfort or power. Back to *a* god—not *the* God. It was then that I took an absolute swan dive back into places of despair and made choices that led back to powerlessness.

One of the first things I did when I returned home from that trip to Wilsonville was contact Slade, my friend from MA. He was one of the few people I'd found who had a similar history of searching for sexual freedom, and I knew that he would be a great source of support. Not only did he understand, but he had also been going through some difficult times since getting out of school. He shared his struggles and how he was finding a lot of clarity in his new relationships within a group he had joined, which I'll call "HOPE Ministries." He introduced me to the head of HOPE and I started attending.

Ministry Academy had led me to incredible places in God's power and demonstration that I never knew existed. It empowered me by discovering and identifying the gifts God had placed inside of me—many of which I found had been dormant before attending the school. It was a place where I was encouraged to dream, and at the school's core was the belief that we aren't on this planet to survive, but to really thrive in Christ. If I had the opportunity, I would go back and do both years all over again. Yet, all the experiences and revelations in school could not address the issues of my heart and character. In order to find sexual wholeness and walk through the intense grief I was battling, I needed personal, one-on-one help. I needed to address the areas of my life where I wasn't spiritually growing.

Once I truly accepted that God's love for me was unwavering and that even amid my worst choices He was still pursuing me, I was free to put down the religious mask of performance and be a mess. I had falsely worn this mask because I believed in the trap that is *comparison*. After school, as I watched my peers step into great roles and ministries, I believed that in comparison my responsibility to my brother was not valuable. My position had changed from student to caregiver, and my obligation was now to put my brother first. I had run with my peers for a time, but when my season suddenly and drastically changed, I believed that I had been disqualified; all this combined with the devastating loss of my father brought me out of the spotlight. In my mind, my value in the eyes of my peers and of God was determined by what I could be seen doing, which meant that my life lost its value. The Apostle Paul talks about this in 1 Corinthians. He likens doing the works of God in order to be seen as drinking milk, and doing the works of God as a good steward and out of love for Him as eating solid food. When my milk jug ran dry I thought the meal was over, despite the fact that there was a heaping plate of solid food right in front of me.

The thing about basing your faith on performance is that you might not know you're doing it until you're no longer given the limelight in which to show off your gifts. God works even through life's tragedies; I don't believe that it was His will that my dad pass away from cancer, but the crisis did cause a great shaking in my walk toward holiness. It was an extremely important time in my life because I learned to ask Him the question: "What is motivating me, and what does my heart need?"

When the mask came off I started meeting with others who were willing to sit as I unraveled my grief, and they offered their words of love. They were able to look past the needs created by my circumstances and see greatness. They saw that my grief was temporary and held my hand as I trudged through it. If there were times that I expected too much of them, they kindly put up boundaries without shaming me for it. For instance, when a lot of this stuff was rising to the surface I sometimes found that it was more intense than I thought I could handle. Scared and with a sense of urgency I would reach out to people, and on a few occasions they didn't have time to see me *immediately*, and had to schedule a time that would work for them. It might sound cold, but not being able to just reach out and grab everything I wanted bolstered my faith that the Lord was never far from me—that seeing them was never the answer, but a resource. Most importantly, during these times they didn't withdraw or dismiss me. I quickly learned that my most valuable relationships were with those who could handle what happened when I took the mask off—when I was most honest and transparent with where I was. They spent many hours with me, just listening with compassion. Then, when I was ready, they challenged me to invite God into the pit. And when I found Him there, He didn't demand that I just "get over it and move on." In fact, it was just the opposite. He revealed to me that He had always been with me as these tragedies occurred in my life. Once I felt the empathy and embrace of God and others I was given the ability to move past my grief. I actually *wanted* to move past it.

I can't stress the importance of these people enough. These few were willing to stop, bandage my wounds, and give me a safe place to heal. They were my good Samaritans, owing me nothing, but valuing me enough to stop and see beyond what I could do for them.

We're told to seek God first and everything else will fall into place, but if you're shackled to grief or condemnation, you don't even know how to approach God. This is where empathetic relationships, pastoral input, and counsel aid to break the bonds that keep us. Empathy says: *I see your pain and your search to find relief in your own way. I understand that struggle; I've walked that road myself. Let's invite God into these places. I will not run for the fear that I might not have all the answers. My job as a believer is to walk alongside you and love you as I point you to Christ.*

If you ever find yourself in a place where you're helping someone deal with grief or other heavy burdens, I hope that the following can be a source of insight. It can be difficult, particularly when you feel you're not suited for it, but there are a few things that will help you keep the focus on God rather than on your own strength.

I spoke about boundaries a bit earlier, and it's an extremely important concept that many people in the Church wrestle with. Boundaries are crucial in reaching out and ministering to others. Growing up in a ministry home with a lack of boundaries—where people were constantly in our house and at our door needing something from us—was taxing to say the least. There were plenty of times when my parents should have said *no*.

It can be hard to tell when to establish a boundary, and I feel that in our attempts to protect our homes and lives from the pressures and demands of others, it's important not to confuse boundaries with barricades. Boundaries allow people appropriate access to a resource; barricades keep them away. Boundaries direct and guide while barricades exclude.

In no way am I trying to be contrary to the many teachings I've heard on boundaries by leaders I greatly respect. Indeed, who you are and what you're called by God to do in life will determine how and where you set your boundaries. I understand that we all have different missions, and these lead us into different spheres of influence in our communities. I find it good practice to ask myself these questions: *Am I demonstrating love all along the way? Are people a means for getting to a destination, or is loving people the destination?*

One important thing to keep in mind when faced with someone in need is that we can't help those who aren't willing to work on their issues. Tearing down all boundaries and over-committing yourself to helping someone whether they like it or not is only going to lead to a lot of pain, confusion, and dependency. And when those people *are* willing to do their part, it's not up to you to dictate how fast they grow. You don't have to micromanage people's lives; just be kind and approachable, even when they're their messiest. And if someone doesn't want help, offer them resources in any way you can and keep the door open for when they hopefully reach a point where they *do* want help.

You won't always have the insight or the time to offer help to someone who asks for it, but you can be available to encourage and direct them to relevant resources. Look past the fear or confusion that comes from a person who asks for more than you can offer. This behavior is just a symptom of what's happening in their life. Those who helped me during this season didn't dismiss me or insist that I meet unrealistic requirements first. If someone gets hit by a car and breaks a leg, are they expected to drive themselves to the hospital? Have empathy and compassion for where people are.

Healing from grief takes a lot of time, love, and consistency, especially for those who have lost close loved ones. Supporting those who are grieving can also be very tasking. The absolute worst thing you can do is cut someone out of your life because you feel that they aren't growing or healing fast enough, or that they're asking for too much time. And to be clear, I'm not speaking just about friendships, but about those times we need to love other believers and sacrifice to see their freedom realized. This may seem oversimplified, but I think it's important to ask God if our boundaries are put up in fear of someone's messiness, or if they're actually there to direct others to a resource, as I talked about.

God's Word says that love is not about *you*. When you love others who can't reciprocate it, you fulfill the law of Christ. Love is an action—a verb. Love is not given on loan. It's given because we were first loved by Him. As Luke 6:32 says, loving those who love you is easy. But people don't have to earn the right to be loved. We are *commanded* to love. Make sure the way you love isn't based on what a person can do for you, and be careful before completely dismissing someone who you think doesn't want help.

In trying to express the importance of unconditional love and of demonstrating boundaries, I'm reminded of one experience in particular. My friend Ashley and I were casual acquaintances through

MA for a while, but a few years later when she heard about my journey she confided in me about her own. She was battling huge problems with alcohol abuse and sexuality. We met for breakfast one day and she poured out the details of her life—the very real, raw, XXX details. My gut reaction was to tie her up, put her in the trunk of my car, take her home, and plead with her until she came to her senses. Obviously this reaction was one of fear.

Instead, I took a breath and forced those reactions to quiet down and my ears to listen. I told her that I cared about her. I also told her that if she wanted to hang out, I wouldn't be willing to drink with her. She knew I had a glass of wine on occasion, like with friends during a dinner party, but I made it clear that I wasn't going to act like I was okay with watching her hammer down beer after beer in order to numb her pain. I wouldn't allow denial to play such a large part in our friendship, and I cared about her enough to make that distinction.

She listened and knew that I cared, but she went on her way, trying to solve her heart needs through whatever means were available. She didn't reach out to me, but my goal was to approach her with kindness. I left the front door open for when she was ready and prayed that she would come to a place where she was willing to let God in again. Making sure that condemnation was far away from our talks was always the goal when we did see each other. I set my hope in God, and not in my ability to have the right answers for her.

A year and lots of prayer later, Ashley finally reached out. She apologized for distancing herself from me and asked if I was willing to help her. She was ready. I was completely ecstatic, though on the outside I played it cool, kind of like the Fonz. (At least that's the way I remember it.) She joined an alcohol rehab program and also the group I was leading at church about sexual purity, and she started to face her pain. Now sober and leading others toward God and sexual wholeness, she is a testimony to love. Many other people loved Ashley, especially during that time in her life, and I just played a small part in reminding her of who she is in Christ.

~ twenty-three ~

Porn and Masturbation

Understanding that the subject of sex—especially as it pertains to women—may be uncomfortable, and also suspecting that some may want to think of my story as a special circumstance, I'd like to suggest that I'm not unique in my struggles.

Growing up in the Church, I observed that the most common mindset regarding the female libido was that it was unimportant and almost nonexistent. A woman's sex drive was hardly spoken about, and when it was brought up in the context of marriage, many women seemed unsatisfied. Sex was a duty, and this left no room for creative expression and passion. Mom's abuse aside, there still existed an overall tone that suggested that sex was bad, passionless, and to be feared.

The lack of conversation about sex, and lack of clarity in the fact that having a sex drive was a normal part of womanhood, aided in much of my confusion. God created sex and called it good, but the lack of this knowledge led to a lot of curiosity on my part. No one seemed to know why we had the rules we did. Waiting for marriage was just what you were supposed to do. Also, celibacy was attributed to purity, but only in the context of waiting for marriage. Nothing was really explained by the people around me; they were more likely to hold that *Don't do it because God said so* philosophy. It wasn't until much later in life that I actually learned why it was important to reserve sex for marriage.

Proverbs 25:2 (MSG) says "God delights in concealing things, whereas scientists delight in discovering things." Imagine kids as little scientists and it's easier to see that as they grow they have a God-given urge to explore. If as a Church we camp in areas of fear and ignorance around subjects that God clearly states are good, we will continue to see generations growing up searching for answers. I applaud and encourage Christians who are willing to step beyond the boundary of taboo the Church has built up around sex, and to educate one another on how we're made and on the value of a healthy sexual relationship in a marriage.

And in all seriousness, I've found that many Christian women are tired of being labeled as low-libido creatures. I think part of this perhaps comes from many Christians wrongly associating the sexual education of women with the feminist movement; they picture man-hating, bra-burning, promiscuous women who want to discard God's design for them. This, again, is fear-based and not reflective of what the Word of God says. Women have high sex drives, just like men do, and that concept is not demonic in nature. How can something God created and gave his seal of approval to be attributed to the demonic? It's only misrepresented in this way when fear is at the base of one's belief system.

The idea of pornography being connected to gender also aids in this misconception. In the Church it seems that the idea of a woman facing the same temptations as a man is unheard of. But time and time again women connect with me in this area only to tell me they've never spoken to anyone about their use of pornography for fear of judgment. These aren't social outcasts. They're not perverted heathens. They're the women that are sitting next to you on Sunday morning. Statistics show a growing number of women who are using pornography on a regular basis. Sin has no gender preference.

HOPE was a group that met once a week for nine months. The format of each session included studying the written materials, listening to a message taught by a married couple, and then breaking into small groups. Even though HOPE was a ministry taught in cells across the country using a unified curriculum, it wasn't the materials from the book that I feel brought freedom to my life. Honestly, the written stuff was always a bit too technical for me to understand. I would stare blankly at it, trying to decode its theological depths and hoping that if I put it under my pillow at night it might seep into my subconscious. It was truly my leaders' pastoral role in my life, along with their biblical knowledge (which they themselves walked out through personal victories) that ministered to me. Do I think there need to be more groups like this? It might be surprising, but I say *no*. My ultimate prayer is that all churches would be led by those equipped to handle issues of morality and sexuality within their congregation without needing to start separate "ministries" for them. It really takes the whole church to love someone who is walking toward wholeness and out of sinful patterns. I'm certainly not knocking HOPE or similar ministries—just looking at the bigger picture and praying for more. In my case, this group was where

God led me. It was a safe place for me to have a conversation about my sexuality, and it was an invaluable resource.

Our group's incredible leaders offered both their time and their counsel to me freely. One of the first key things I learned at HOPE was that my errant sexual desires were not *problems*; they were *symptoms*. With that mentality, as I repented (changed my mind) about how I was going to meet my needs and invite God's grace into those areas, I began to see huge shifts in my heart and in my thinking process. My relationships with those who had also walked this road supplied me with a faith-building understanding that God was approachable in *all* areas of my life. The leaders allowed me to ask the hard questions. In fact, they encouraged it. And one of my questions was: Why is masturbation discouraged outside of marriage?

Yup. Masturbation. We're talking about that now. I've found that sometimes, even in situations of openness regarding sexual temptation and pornography, that word is still just a little too taboo to use. It's sort of suggested, but not actually said. And just like with pornography, the idea of it not being exclusively for men will come as a surprise to a lot of people. In HOPE, however, everything was fair game.

I asked why masturbation was a bad idea if it was a biological release. In fact, the Bible is pretty explicit about a lot of sins, but doesn't really cover this topic directly. If it wasn't explicitly a sin, why was it considered a bad thing? Yet another question that, growing up, would have likely been answered with, "Just don't do it, that's why."

What I learned is that masturbation was not in God's plan for me because it was ultimately a form of self-centeredness, which only aided in the isolation I felt so strongly. Sex was meant to be shared. My biological drives were tied to my mental ones, and they could be directed in other ways. There was never any denying that I had a sex drive that seemed to talk all the time, but the lie I believed was that it had to be answered my way. I learned that when I was taking care of myself, eating well, working out, and engaging in healthy activities and relationships, I could manage my sex drive. Understanding anatomy and learning how my body was made also helped remove some of the mystique that made masturbation more desirable. This all allowed me to stay ahead of my drive.

Take away all the taboo crazy church talk about going blind or growing hair on your palms; take away all the fear tactics. Once people could speak logically into that area of my life it was easy to see why it wasn't God's best for me. I could see that by its very nature it tied into a fantasy life that had no bearing on reality, whether it was connected to pornography or not. All it took was a bit of openness and suddenly I could see the issue clearly, after years and years of struggling and feeling nothing but shame and confusion. But like all things, of course, that didn't mean that the problem was solved; I had to develop new habits while breaking spiritual bonds.

Before, when I used pornography, my routine went something like this: "Okay Jesus, so I'm going to go into this room over here. You're not going to be happy about what's taking place in there, so I won't involve you in this transaction. There's soda in the fridge, please help yourself and make yourself comfortable. I'll be right back." Then I would go into that room, and it would lead to days of condemnation, which would then lead me back to hopelessness, and eventually start the whole process all over again.

At HOPE I learned that the reason I repeated this cycle was that He wasn't allowed in the room with me. I remember the first time one of the leaders brought this revelation to me regarding the area of compulsive masturbation. By that point I was choosing not to view porn, but there was still a drive to comfort myself through masturbation, and the images that I'd viewed over the years were still easily recalled. When I brought up the subject my leader said, "Liz, the next time you're going to masturbate, try inviting the Holy Spirit to speak to you. He can't bring freedom if you keep Him out of this area."

My first response of course was to run right out of the office, as far away from these crazy people as possible. I mean, what on Earth was she smoking? Once I had left and processed the information though, my fear subsided and I realized that it really *was* the next step in getting free. Because of that advice and how true it rang in my heart, I found that I no longer *could* keep Jesus in the other room. He simply had to have access to my heart and actions. I had to let go of my fear that He would take something away and impose rules upon me without giving me the means to see obedience through. Jesus is freedom, and where He is, freedom follows. I had to invite God to speak to me where I most experienced separation from Him. I saw that my pride in thinking that I could work through this obstacle in my own way had been keeping me from repentance.

With these new changes in place, I received grace. The compulsion subsided and my relationship with God deepened; it was pride exchanged for trust. There was a new peace within those areas of compulsion, and I had a choice to either receive it or deny it.

There was something else I needed in all this, and it goes hand-in-hand with repentance: I had to be obedient in what I felt He was saying and in what the Word says. Obedience is not a popular word, but it's required to receive freedom from sin—doing something that God asks of you regardless of whether you understand it or of whether you feel you can do it.

For me, being obedient meant giving up substances and outwardly things (other gods) that I was going to for power and comfort. I had to die to my old self-centered patterns and receive my new identity by inviting God into areas of shame, being absolutely honest with Him, and receiving the grace and direction I needed to move past those areas. Obedience is extremely important to remember, because ultimately the choice in all this was always mine. In order to break free of this false identity I'd believed, I had to make the decision to stop. Whether to continue to grow or to turn away from truth was, and still is, *always* my choice.

In Matthew 7:13-14 (AMP) Jesus speaks about the narrow way. (13) "Enter through the narrow gate, for wide is the gate and spacious and broad is the way that leads away to destruction, and many are those who are entering through it." (14) "But the gate is narrow (contracted by pressure) and the way is straitened and compressed that leads away to life, and few are those who find it."

Yielding to God with all of my heart produced a lot of pressure because that road is narrow, putting the squeeze on all the things that I was carrying with me into His presence. I had compulsively masturbated since a young age, and had adopted pornography in my high school years, but I can say that since reaching the point where I surrendered to this process in complete relationship with God, I've been free. No matter where you're at, there are always two choices, and I could go back tomorrow if I chose to. Holiness is a road, not a destination. But after living life with a renewed mind for so long, pornography no longer has power over me. I've invested too much into my relationship with Him to go back to such destructive and isolating patterns. There's now so much more in my life to live for and look forward to.

~ twenty-four ~

Same-Sex Attraction

In dealing with my pattern of pornography and masturbation, HOPE also gave me a place to address questions about same-sex attraction.

Just to be clear, HOPE was not a conversion therapy group. For those of you who don't know what conversion therapy is (also known as reparative therapy), very often it's a therapy designed to change sexual orientation from homosexual to heterosexual.

I'll admit that I'm skeptical of such therapy. I feel it can sometimes treat homosexuality as an illness that needs to be *cured*, and I feel that's unbiblical. A common misconception within the Church is that your identity rests in your sexual expression, but the truth is that sexuality is only one part that makes up the greater whole of your life. I feel that sometimes conversion therapy is coming at the issue as though the goal of the Christian faith is to be heterosexual, whereas it's actually to be reconciled with God through Jesus Christ and receive the identity *He* made for you.

I can't make any broad statements, however, because there are many different methods used in conversion therapy. Altogether it's just too large a topic to go into here. In dealing with these issues I would just be wary of any therapy that puts an emphasis on the therapist or on grunt work meant to *fix* you, rather than on actually taking the whole thing to God while living a sanctified life.

The Bible gives two options for expressing your sexuality when you are a believer: celibacy and heterosexual marriage. Sex is a gift that can be given in marriage, or quieted through the grace of God in celibacy. It's a choice, and despite what many people seem to think, God does not require that we marry in order to lead meaningful, fulfilling lives. Nor does He require those who may have previously identified as homosexual to live a celibate life as a result. It's important to create an atmosphere in our churches in which both celibacy and marriage are accepted so that as people are walking out their journey with God, they're free from unnecessary expectations and pressures that could hinder them. An atmosphere where our lives center on Christ and not marital status.

As Christians, we have to recognize that sexuality is temporal and refocus on what is eternal. The purpose is always to reconcile with Christ, which produces holiness through a disciplined life—not to forcefully develop heterosexual thought patterns and behavior traits.

With all that said, the counseling I received regarding my sexuality in HOPE helped me identify and uncover my misconceptions, many of which came from growing up in an atmosphere where sex was shameful.

To be clear, I'm not a victim of my upbringing or my childhood. To think that would be counter-productive, as the victim mentality is just another form of self-enabled powerlessness. Ultimately, I chose to seek refuge from my pain in my own way, which was often the way of sin. Upbringing plays a vital role in our views and understanding of sex, but there are plenty of people who identify as homosexual who grew up with loving parents and open talks about sex. Basically, I believe it's important to never generalize or place all the blame on one thing, as everybody's experiences and root sins are different.

I received a lot of insight into one aspect of my same-sex attraction: how I viewed my own femininity. I touched on this earlier, and HOPE was really when it all came to light. I'd attempted to fix my emotional needs with sexual expression, and as a result my approach to relationships became twisted. The women I were attracted to held the power or companionship that I longed for, and through them my soul tried to consume what it needed. It was always the same pattern: they were strong, knew how to deliver, and their emotions took a back seat (or at least that was what I perceived). This was the opposite of how I saw myself. These women became another god for me to obsess over. Basically, it was idolatry.

The further I traveled on this journey the more I realized that my expressions of femininity were not forms of powerlessness. I no longer had to strip away all things feminine in order to protect myself. Shortly after returning to God and ending my sexual relationships with women, my appearance and demeanor slowly softened and changed, but my heart still hated the powerlessness I felt in being female. It took time for God to fully reveal that He created me to have a voice, to lead others with love, and to be confident in Him—that I was not powerless or voiceless because of what He built in me. I was to be the opposite of what I'd lived as for years: an insecure woman, grasping for value and attention, all the while being dehumanized. My feminine nature is now a source of strength; my ability to respond to and nurture others is very powerful.

I accepted how God made me, and as temptations would continue to arise regarding same-sex attraction, I would take them to God with an honest conversation. It wasn't until I stopped acting upon those temptations (sex with others or with myself through fantasy) that the strong desires subsided and it became clear where this compulsion to idolize was rooted. Sometimes this process was messy and unclear, but I worked through it by being obedient and choosing to focus on Him. Again, that obedience is important. I've stressed many times that my sinful actions never really removed my access to God, but at the same time, in order to find freedom in my actions (and to keep that freedom), I had to center on my love for Him first and foremost. This new pattern of forthrightly relating to God revealed depths of His love that I had never even fathomed. The good news of the gospel was now alive and working freely in my life. The old broken images that had once caught my attention no longer captivated me. With this new identity settling in me, the attraction to women lost its hook.

I know now that if there is a temptation, I'm to ask the Holy Spirit if I'm believing a lie about my identity, and what my heart needs from Him. Is this some sort of bippity-boppity-boo magic self-help mind trick? Nope. It's a way to remind myself of what the Word of God says about me and that what He speaks to me day-to-day is truth.

If I now feel drawn to a woman, often the Lord reveals the qualities in her that I'm admiring, and that He's building in me. No longer do I sexualize women in order to obtain what I'm searching for. Being drawn or attracted to someone's qualities is not a sin. It's what I might do with the temptation to sexualize a person that's a sin, because it puts that person in the place of God. No longer do I use women as an object to find meaning; now my relationships are ones of friendship and mentorship alone. This is key for not only those who face same-sex attraction, but also for heterosexual attraction outside the boundaries God has established. There is no magic prayer or trick to all this—just the long process of walking out holiness. Today I better understand the nature of my temptation, and because of that, its power is miniscule compared to ten or fifteen years ago.

What I think is difficult for many churches to accept is the reality that people who face same-sex attraction (or other sexual sin for that matter) probably aren't going to have a wham-bam-thank-you-ma'am one-time deliverance moment. Don't get me wrong; we should totally expect strong, eventful encounters with God's power in which truth whacks us in the face and spiritual oppression leaves. But thinking that this instant deliverance fixes relational patterns denies the role that repentance and renewing of the mind play in the process of restoration. Yes, sexual sin is as forgivable as any other sin, but the damage it does is relational. That damage has to be healed as well—not only the damage to your relationship with God, but to how you view, interact with, and relate to others. In my years of mentoring women in the Church and encouraging friends who deal with these issues of sexual sin, I haven't met one person who's had an instant encounter with God that took away all temptation. The renewing of the mind through repentance is a working process, and one that is our own responsibility to engage in.

Even though I am indeed married, let me also say that marriage is not a *cure* for single people who struggle with same-sex attraction. The same goes for anyone struggling with pornography for that matter. It's all-too-common for well-meaning but misguided leaders to pressure others with issues of sexual identity or sexual sin to marry in order to offer a quick fix, or to "make it legal," so to speak. Particularly here in America we want to get rich quick, to make dinner in just five microwave minutes, to throw some paint on it and call it done. Are you a man, feeling attracted to other men? Well slap a ring on the first lady you see and BAM, you're good to go! Problem solved.

Yeesh. This can't be further away from the right strategy. If you're single and you've got problems with pornography, fantasizing, masturbating, or other self-control issues—whether it's all focused on same-sex attraction or not—finding a finger to slap a ring onto is the *last* thing you need to do. Marriage compounds these issues; it does not resolve them. That kind of relationship only puts the pressure on and brings more people into the equation who can be hurt. Outward acts never solve inner turmoil. Don't get me wrong; if you're already married and struggling there is definitely hope. But if not, don't think you can throw a coat of paint on your life and call it good.

Overall I just feel that this is an area where there's a lot of room for growth. It can be difficult for people struggling with these issues to see freedom because too few of us are willing to sit with them. It's awkward, it's messy, and it's just uncomfortable for everyone involved. But Jesus tells us in Luke 10 that the workers are few but the harvest is plentiful. We may feel ill-equipped to help someone in a situation like this, but it's important to act on the faith that ultimately, He will provide.

~ twenty-five ~

LGBT and the Church

The biggest risk in writing a book on this topic is that well-meaning believers might use it as a weapon instead of a means for conversation. My heart in writing it is not only to reach out to those who struggle in the Church, but also to aid in bridging the divide of pain between the Christian community and those who identify as LGBT (lesbian, gay, bisexual and transgender) by providing an empathetic point of view and encouraging a new perspective on how to love others. Because honestly, we're losing the battle; we're losing our ability to love because of our fear, judgment, and lack of knowledge.

I'd like to address two modes of thought I feel are dominating the Church view—at least in America—of the LGBT community. I believe these modes are hindering our ability to love, disciple, and correctly demonstrate Christ. Many Christians view the LGBT community with either Disdain or Approval, and both mindsets are unbiblical and ignore the work of the Cross.

Disdain regarding the LGBT community adopts the notion that there is an "us" and a "them." The "us and them" mentality goes something like this: "You (gays, lesbians, etc.) are the reason why America is going to Hell in a hand basket! You disgust me! Keep away from my sweet, innocent children!" People with this mindset are preoccupied with what they tout as the *gay agenda* and the idea that politics can be used to enforce moral standards. The practice of publicly "fighting" against the gay community, such as through social media outlets, fails to set a tone that will invite conversation and strengthen friendships.

The idea that God was unapproachable because of my choices was the biggest lie that kept me from Him, so when we Christians harbor this Disdain, we've obviously lost sight of the power of the Cross at work in our own lives. It's a poisonous mentality that a person has to meet God's requirements in order to be loved and respected, because that expectation then spills over into our own relationships as well. The whole world around us becomes unapproachable because it doesn't fit perfectly into our own little world, and thus we not only withhold love, but we broadcast hate. It's the mask of religion, and it's downright pharisaical.

Romans 3:23 (NIV) says, "…for all have sinned and fall short of the glory of God." It's only through Jesus that we can come to God, who calls us sons and daughters. This isn't through any act of ourselves, but through the Cross. We all have our roads to Damascus; some are just shorter than others.

With that said, I urge believers to carefully weigh what they bring to society in regards to their opinions of the LGBT community. Hate, judgment, harshness, rudeness, and disrespect have *never* won someone over to Christ. Not once. We cannot change others; that's impossible. It's only by representing the work God has done in us that we can point others to Him. It's only those who resist the work of holiness in their own lives who can somehow validate their judgment of sin in others. It's much easier to project our own failings onto others rather than initiate a loving relationship with those who live differently than we do. The fruit of loving others grows only from our own holiness.

I believe that America's primary problem is not that it's suffering under the hand of a *gay agenda*; it's suffering from a Church with an identity issue. Much of what believers call the gay agenda is the unpaid bill of the Church. The Church has attempted to broadcast judgment in public settings instead of engaging privately in loving, truthful conversations through relationships. Public ridicule and rejection is not the gospel. To radically love others the way Christ loves us requires relationships with those who do not know Him. I'm not denying that there are spiritual forces at war with God's plan, but at the root of it all *we* stand responsible for how we love others. And for too long we as a Church have been reactionary when faced with things we don't understand. We need to learn to listen to the cries of others' hearts.

Using terminologies and slogans to establish a sort of mantra with which we can mock an entire people group is not only ineffective, but is most definitely not the good news of the gospel. Saying "It's Adam and Eve, not Adam and Steve" does absolutely nothing but communicate to the LGBT community that we don't understand or even wish to understand the world they live in. I constantly hear the most ridiculous stuff, like, "The rainbow was ours first, and we need to take it back for

Jesus!" First of all, the rainbow flag exists in other countries and holds other symbolic meanings. The rainbow was never *ours* to possess. It was given to God's people as a promise. Does the rainbow in the Word not represent victory and the promise of grace? Second, here's an idea: Every time you see the rainbow flag, perhaps use it as a reminder to love the person sporting it. Maybe even pray a blessing over that person's life. And if they're in any way connected to you, consider building a relationship.

The second group of Christians who I believe to be in error regarding their approach to the LGBT community is that which meets it with Approval—with the idea that it is God-ordained to set your identity in your sexual expression. These believers are trying to bridge the gap that the Church has created through fear and ignorance, which is a truly noble thing. But I feel that 2 Timothy 3:5 illustrates it well; this is having a form of godliness but denying its power. I believe those who want to see the ostracizing of a community diminish at *all* costs are losing their witness by changing the gospel. This mindset denies the fact that *every* part of our lives must be given to God in order for us to walk in holiness. It desires unity over the truth and overlooks the fact that we are all born into sin, and that it's through our relationship with Christ that we become a *new* creation. Our culture defines people by their sexual identity, which is temporal, and the gospel defines people by their reconciliation with God, which is eternal.

When we come at the issue from this angle of absolute Approval, the Christian life is limited to the power of the community that surrounds it. It's limited to gathering around our own definitions of God instead of actually hearing and responding to how God defines Himself and us. Those who see the Bible as an outdated and failing source will often carry these mindsets. This reduces the gospel to only a part of its purpose, which is to reach out to the disenfranchised, lonely, rejected, misunderstood, and the discarded. It turns Christianity into a mere club to belong to, where we gather around our comfort in each other rather than The One Who Comforts.

Rejection, isolation and loneliness are real issues. There is no denying that at the core of all humanity is a desire to be loved and to belong. However, believing that the gospel of Christ is solely based on a living community becomes its own sort of false god. It's a half truth. Healthy Christian community is vital to protect and provide a safe place while you reconcile with God and receive love from others, but it cannot replace Him. If it could, then Jesus didn't really have to die.

twenty-six

Unwavering Love

As ambassadors of Christ, the primary stance I believe we are called to take—regardless of a person's beliefs—is one of love and respect. There is no denying that this gap between the Church and the LGBT community is littered with casualties. There have been uncountable missed opportunities to love others throughout the years, and I believe that these have only aided in escalating this war. Your words and actions carry power. Let's get our information from sitting with people instead of from what gossip and the media tell us.

It's by our own personal victories over sin that we will become a light to the world. Face sin and compromise in your own life, and people will be drawn to your light. I think Matthew 7:5 (NKJV) is very fitting here: "...First remove the plank from your own eye, and then you will see clearly to remove the speck from your brother's eye." You've got to clear your own vision before you can help others.

My father loved me. He was not violent, hateful, demoralizing, or condemning. He also didn't embrace every decision I made and tell me I was expressing myself from a Godly perspective. If he had taken either stance, there's a very good chance that I would have never had the slightest inkling to run to God for help—and right now, instead of writing this book, I would be a chain-smoking lesbian biker chick, growing pot in the woods of Northern California. (Hey, it could have happened!) Instead he continued to love me as he held to the truth of the gospel.

Be the Good Samaritan, eat with the tax collector, and die to your own sin. "By their fruit you will recognize them." - Matthew 7:16 (NIV)

I've covered a lot of areas in this book, but my central goal has always been to demonstrate how love and respect are the keys to inviting others into a relationship with Jesus. And it's not just in regards to the LGBT community, but to literally *everyone,* however we want to identify them: homosexuals, drug users, atheists, Muslims, insurance salesmen, the guy who picks up your recycling every week—*it doesn't matter*! We all erect walls around ourselves because of fear, and I want to encourage you to question why they're there, and to tear them down.

Even during the process of writing this book I've spoken with people about it, and surprised them with the story of my struggles. And when they learn about this aspect of my life, I often find that they're incredibly interested to hear more. The places I've been are so foreign to some that they find it fascinating, having never had the opportunity to sit and ask questions on these subjects. With knowledge and understanding comes wisdom, and deep down people are hungry to bridge this gap between "us and them," whoever "they" may be. I want this book to be a resource, a conversation-starter, a source of knowledge, and an invitation to view the people of the world as *exactly* what they are: God's creation.

This is the good news, Christians. This isn't the latest and greatest message that I'm using to sell books. It won't go out of style when the next thing comes around in a few years. This is the *oldest* message. He died so we can live. We die so He can live in us. He loves us first so we can love others.

Jesus broke bread with a prostitute. In His dying moments a murderer saw Him as the Christ, and He welcomed the man into Paradise. He sat with and ministered to the broken, the hopeless, those who were so entrenched in sin that the rest of society wanted nothing to do with them. We are given explicit permission to sit with people of all walks of life, just as Jesus did. We have permission to love.

And God's love is at the very heart of my message. It's how we're able to reach any community, it's how He was able to reach me, and ultimately it's the reason He sent His son to die on the cross for us. He made the ultimate sacrifice as one all-encompassing act of love so that we could multiply and perpetuate it in our own lives. And this love He gave us will never waver, never lessen, never end; He *is* love. No matter who you are, there is always a kind, adventurous, funny, loving God waiting for you with open arms.

It's a narrow path, but if you take His hand He'll walk with you every step of the way.

Epilogue

I'm sitting in pre-service prayer, which is held in a smaller room off of the main sanctuary. It's about an hour before service starts, and as usual the peaceful atmosphere of the room gives me the perfect opportunity to relax and talk to God.

It's been two months since the incident at the bar, and since then my world has begun to right itself. I've been connecting with my mentors, discovering great truths about myself, and delving deeper into my relationship with God than I ever could have dreamed. I reflect on all this as I sit, my head bowed and my eyes closed, just listening to the worship music coming through the sound system and enjoying the presence of God.

I'm slightly annoyed when two guys come and sit a few spaces to my right. There are a lot of empty chairs in the room, and these guys could have picked any of them. I ignore this, however, and get out my Bible. I read a few highlighted passages, thumb between bookmarks and begin to settle again…until I hear something that cuts through my brain like nails on a chalkboard. I glance over and notice that the guy closest to me is eating a muffin. *Loudly.*

Loud eating has always been a very large pet peeve of mine, so this further breaks my concentration and the peaceful atmosphere. I try to ignore it, but to no avail. Who is this guy? Can't he see I'm trying to pray, here?

After a while the two guys start talking, and I find that Mr. Muffin has a charming British accent. Suddenly I forget all about the smacking noises. I send another glance his way, and this time I notice that he's cute. *Really* cute. I continue to thumb through my Bible, though by now my concentration is officially broken.

After a while one of the leaders comes to the front of the room and asks us to pair up with someone we haven't met so we can pray for each other. Acting quickly I turn to my right, only to find him already looking at me with a smile.

"Hi," he said, "my name's Andy."

But what came next is a story for another day.